Stan Dolan

Discrete Mathematics
For AQA

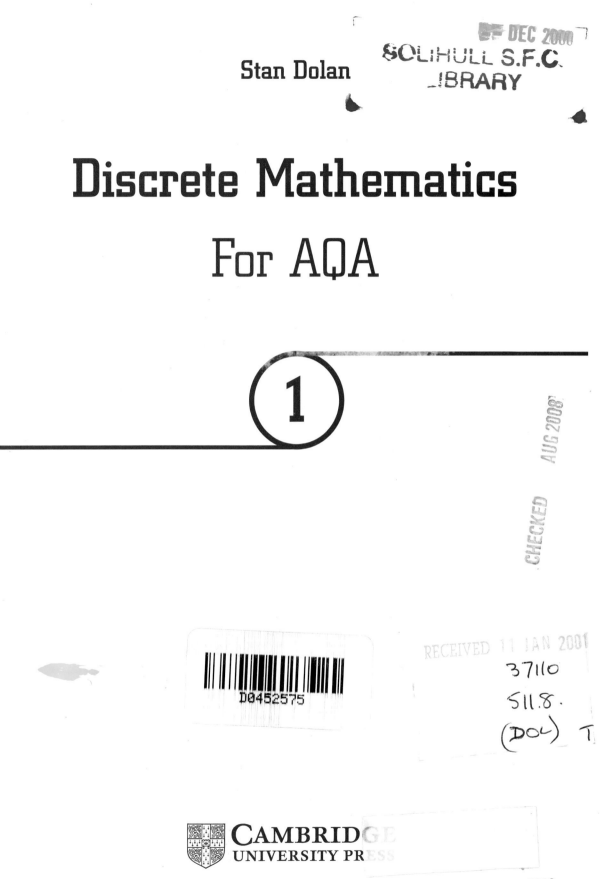

1

CAMBRIDGE
UNIVERSITY PRESS

PUBLISHED BY THE PRESS SYNDICATE OF THE UNIVERSITY OF CAMBRIDGE
The Pitt Building, Trumpington Street, Cambridge, United Kingdom

CAMBRIDGE UNIVERSITY PRESS
The Edinburgh Building, Cambridge CB2 2RU, UK
40 West 20th Street, New York, NY 10011-4211, USA
10 Stamford Road, Oakleigh, VIC 3166, Australia
Ruiz de Alarcón 13, 28014 Madrid, Spain
Dock House, The Waterfront, Cape Town 8001, South Africa

http://www.cambridge.org

© Cambridge University Press 2000

First published 2000

Printed in the United Kingdom by Redwood Books, Trowbridge

Typefaces Times, Helvetica   *Systems* Microsoft® Word, MathType™

A catalogue record for this book is available from the British Library

ISBN 0 521 79941 4 paperback

Cover image © DigitalVision

Contents

Introduction

This book has been written for the Discrete Mathematics module, D1, of AQA Specification A.

The book is divided into chapters roughly corresponding to specification headings. Occasionally a section includes an important result that is difficult to prove or outside the specification. These sections are marked with an asterisk (*) in the section heading, and there is usually a sentence early on explaining precisely what it is that the student needs to know.

It is important to recognise that, while every effort has been made by the author and by AQA to make the books match the specification, the books do not and must not define the examination. It is conceivable that questions might be asked in the examination, examples of which do not appear specifically in the books.

Occasionally within the text paragraphs appear in this type style. These paragraphs are usually outside the main stream of the mathematical argument, but may help to give insight, or suggest extra work or different approaches.

Numerical work is presented in a form intended to discourage premature approximation. In ongoing calculations inexact numbers appear in decimal form like 3.456..., signifying that the number is held in a calculator to more places than are given. Numbers are not rounded at this stage; the full display could be either 3.456 123 or 3.456 789. Final answers are then stated with some indication that they are approximate, for example '1.23 correct to 3 significant figures'.

There are plenty of exercises, and each chapter contains a Miscellaneous exercise which includes examination questions. Most of these questions were set in AQA examinations, and some were set in OCR examinations. Questions which go beyond examination requirements are marked by an asterisk. At the end of the book there is a set of Revision exercises and two practice examination papers. The author thanks Jan Dangerfield, who contributed to the exercises, and Hugh Neill, both of whom read the book very carefully and made many extremely useful and constructive comments.

AQA(AEB) and AQA(NEAB) examination questions are reproduced by permission of the Assessment and Qualifications Alliance.

The author thanks AQA and Cambridge University Press for their help in producing this book.

1 Algorithms

This chapter looks at the meaning of 'Discrete Mathematics' and introduces some algorithms. When you have completed it you should

- know what an algorithm is
- be able to apply the algorithms known as Bubble Sort, Shuttle Sort, Shell Sort and Quicksort
- know what is meant by correctness, finiteness, generality and stopping conditions.

1.1 What is Discrete Mathematics?

You will have already met, in Statistics, the distinction between continuous and discrete data. Continuous data can take any value in a numerical range: measurements of height, weight and time all produce continuous data. Discrete data can only take values which are strictly separated from each other: measurements of the number of children in a family or the number of letters in a word are discrete data which take only whole-number values.

In the 17th century, Sir Isaac Newton and other leading mathematicians started the development of calculus, which deals specifically with continuous data, and graphs which are generally smooth. Discrete Mathematics deals only with branches of mathematics which do *not* employ the continuous methods of calculus.

However, the distinction between continuous and discrete sometimes becomes blurred. For example, computers essentially deal in Discrete Mathematics, because they hold numbers using sequences of 1s and 0s, and can only hold a finite amount of information. However, advanced computers can work to a very high degree of accuracy, and can do very good approximations to continuous mathematics. They can give approximate solutions to equations which otherwise could not be solved.

Computer screens are divided into 'pixels' (the word is a contraction of 'picture elements'), and so computer and TV screens are essentially discrete devices. However, because the discrete pixels are so small, the images on the screen appear continuous.

But all this is only part of the definition of Discrete Mathematics. It is also widely (but not universally) accepted that Discrete Mathematics is restricted to branches of mathematics whose development has mainly been in the 20th century. It is no coincidence that its importance and application have arisen in the same period of history as the development of computers.

Part of working with computers is the idea of a procedure, or 'algorithm', to solve a problem. You probably know an algorithm which enables you to find the answer to a long multiplication given the two numbers you wish to multiply. Algorithms form a substantial part of Discrete Mathematics. In this course, most of the algorithms will be topics related to the best use of time and resources. These have applications in industry, business, computing and in military matters.

1.2 Following instructions

An algorithm is a sequence of instructions which, if followed correctly, allows anyone to solve a problem.

The mathematics problems studied in school tend to be those for which previous generations of mathematicians have already worked out the appropriate sequences of instructions. For example, consider this algorithm for finding the median of a set of numbers.

Find the median		*Example* 12, 2, 3, 8, 2, 4
Step 1	Arrange the numbers in ascending order.	2 2 3 4 8 12
Step 2	Delete the end numbers.	2 3 4 8
Step 3	Repeat Step 2 until only one or two numbers remain.	3 4
Step 4	The median is the number that remains, or the average of the two numbers that remain.	3.5

It is especially important to think of mathematical procedures as sequences of precise instructions when you are programming a computer to solve a problem. Computer programs are algorithms written in a language which a computer can interpret.

Other types of everyday algorithm include cookery recipes, explanations on how to set up video recorders, and assembly instructions for flat-pack furniture. The following paragraph, from some instructions recently followed by the author, illustrates some of the advantages and disadvantages of algorithmic methods.

> From Bag 46 take one $\frac{3}{8}" \times 2\frac{1}{2}"$ Hex Head Bolt and one $\frac{3}{8}"$ Nyloc Nut. Insert the bolt through the bottom hole of the bracket on part 1050 and through the hole in part 1241. Attach the Nyloc Nut finger tight.

Providing the instructions are sufficiently precise, you can carefully work through an algorithm such as this one without needing to fully understand how everything fits together. Similarly, you can follow mathematical algorithms by rote, without understanding the process.

However, if you do understand a process then you can adapt the basic algorithm to special features of the problem, and thereby solve the problem more efficiently. Just as the author eventually stopped needing detailed instructions on how to attach parts together with appropriate-sized nuts and bolts, so you would not need to follow the algorithm slavishly if asked to find the median of $\overbrace{2, 2, 2, \ldots, 2}^{1000 \text{ numbers}}$.

> An **algorithm** is a finite sequence of instructions for solving a problem. It enables a person or a computer to solve the problem without needing to understand the whole process.

You might wonder why the word 'finite' is necessary. The reason is that there are processes which are essentially infinite, like finding the sum of a series such as

$$1 + \frac{1}{2} + \frac{1}{4} + \frac{1}{8} + \ldots$$

by adding successive terms to the 'sum so far'. This never ends, and is not an algorithm.

In this book you will learn some algorithms which have been developed to solve particular problems in Discrete Mathematics. You will need to know how to carry these algorithms out by hand, although most real-world applications involve so many steps that they require the use of a computer. You will also need to have some idea of why the methods work.

1.3 Sorting algorithms

Any collection of data, such as a telephone directory, is only of value if information can be found quickly when needed. Alongside the development of computer databases, many algorithms have been developed to speed up the modification, deletion, addition and retrieval of data. This section will consider just one aspect of this, the sorting of a list of numbers into numerical order.

There is no single 'best' algorithm for sorting. The size of the data set, and how muddled up it is initially, both affect which algorithm will sort the data most efficiently.

Bubble Sort
This algorithm is so called because the smaller numbers gradually rise up the list like bubbles in a glass of lemonade. The algorithm depends upon successive comparisons of pairs of numbers, as follows.

- Compare the 1st and 2nd numbers in the list, and swap them if the 2nd number is smaller.
- Compare the 2nd and 3rd numbers and swap if the 3rd is smaller.
- Continue in this way through the entire list.

Consider the application of this procedure, called a **pass**, to the list of numbers

5, 1, 2, 6, 9, 4, 3.

The numbers are first placed vertically in the left column. After each comparison the list is rewritten to the right. Fig. 1.1 shows one pass of Bubble Sort.

You can see that this pass has required 6 comparisons and 4 swaps.

Original list						New list
5	1	1	1	1	1	1
1	5	2	2	2	2	2
2	2	5	5	5	5	5
6	6	6	6	6	6	6
9	9	9	9	9	4	4
4	4	4	4	4	9	3
3	3	3	3	3	3	9

Fig. 1.1

The result of this pass through the list is that the numbers 1, 2, 4 and 3 (the bubbles) have each moved up one place. The other numbers have either stayed in place or moved down. In particular, you should be able to see that the largest number (in this case the 9) will always move to the bottom.

The complete Bubble Sort algorithm can be written as follows.

Bubble Sort

Step 1 If there is only one number in the list then stop.

Step 2 Make one pass down the list, comparing numbers in pairs and swapping as necessary.

Step 3 If no swaps have occurred then stop. Otherwise, ignore the last element of the list and return to Step 1.

Original list	1st pass	2nd pass	3rd pass	4th pass	5th pass
5	1	1	1	1	1
1	2	2	2	2	2
2	5	5	4	3	3
6	6	4	3	4	4
9	4	3	5	5	5
4	3	6	6	6	6
3	9	9	9	9	9

Fig. 1.2

Each pass alters the list of numbers as in Fig. 1.2, and the list ends up in order. The numbers under the 'steps' are the ones that are ignored.

Table 1.3 shows the numbers of swaps and comparisons which are required at each pass.

	1st pass	2nd pass	3rd pass	4th pass	5th pass	Totals
Comparisons	6	5	4	3	2	20
Swaps	4	2	2	1	0	9

Table 1.3

One disadvantage of Bubble Sort is that once the data have been sorted, another complete pass through the data is necessary to ensure that the sorting has been finished. The next algorithm partially overcomes this problem.

Shuttle Sort

This algorithm is so called because numbers can move up more than one place in a pass.

Shuttle Sort

1st pass Compare the 1st and 2nd numbers in the list and swap if necessary.

2nd pass Compare the 2nd and 3rd numbers in the list and swap if necessary. If a swap has occurred, compare the 1st and 2nd numbers and swap if necessary.

3rd pass Compare the 3rd and 4th numbers in the list and swap if necessary. If a swap has occurred, compare the 2nd and 3rd numbers, and so on up the list.

And so on, through the entire list.

The results of successive passes of Shuttle Sort on the list

5, 1, 2, 6, 9, 4, 3

are shown in Fig. 1.4. The numbers above the stepped line are those which have been compared at each pass.

Original list	1st pass	2nd pass	3rd pass	4th pass	5th pass	6th pass
5	1	1	1	1	1	1
1	5	2	2	2	2	2
2	2	5	5	5	4	3
6	6	6	6	6	5	4
9	9	9	9	9	6	5
4	4	4	4	4	9	6
3	3	3	3	3	3	9

Fig. 1.4

Table 1.5 shows the numbers of swaps and comparisons which are required at each pass of Shuttle Sort.

	1st pass	2nd pass	3rd pass	4th pass	5th pass	6th pass	Totals
Comparisons	1	2	1	1	4	5	14
Swaps	1	1	0	0	3	4	9

Table 1.5

Shuttle Sort has involved the same number of swaps as Bubble Sort, but far fewer comparisons: 14 as opposed to 20.

Exercise 1A

1 (a) Apply Bubble Sort to the reverse-ordered list 5, 4, 3, 2, 1. Keep a count of the number of comparisons and swaps.

(b) Apply Shuttle Sort to the list 5, 4, 3, 2, 1. Again, keep a count of the number of comparisons and swaps.

(c) Compare the two sorting algorithms for lists in reverse order.

2 (a) Apply Bubble Sort to a list of 6 numbers. What is the maximum possible number of comparisons and swaps that would need to be made for a list of 6 numbers?

(b) Generalise your answer to part (a) for a list of n numbers.

3 Apply Shuttle Sort to the list 4, 1, 6, 8, 2. Show the result of each pass and keep a count of the number of comparisons and swaps.

4 Another sorting algorithm, called the Interchange algorithm, is defined as follows.

Step 1 If there is only one number in the list then stop.

Step 2 Find the smallest number in the list and interchange it with the first number.

Step 3 Ignore the first element of the list and return to Step 1.

(a) Write down your own sub-algorithm to 'find the smallest number in a list'. How many comparisons are needed when applying your algorithm to a list containing n numbers?

(b) How many comparisons and swaps are needed when applying the Interchange algorithm to the list 5, 4, 3, 2, 1?

5 Here are two algorithms. In each case, find the output if $m = 4$ and $n = 3$, and decide whether the algorithm would still work if either or both m and n were negative.

(a) **Step 1** Read the positive integers m and n.
   Step 2 Replace m by $m-1$, and n by $n+1$.
   Step 3 If $m > 0$, go to Step 2. Otherwise write n.

(b) **Step 1** Read the positive integers m and n.
   Step 2 Let $p = 0$.
   Step 3 Replace m by $m-1$, and p by $p+n$.
   Step 4 If $m > 0$, go to Step 3. Otherwise write p.

1.4 Some important terms

You have already met the idea of finiteness; that is, an algorithm must stop after a finite number of steps. An even more fundamental idea is that of **correctness**, that is, the algorithm does actually do what it is intended to do!

Example 1.4.1

The following algorithm is designed to produce a sequence of N prime numbers.

   Step 1 Read N.
   Step 2 Let $X = 1$.
   Step 3 Let $P = X + 1$.
   Step 4 Print P.
   Step 5 Replace X by $X \times P$.
   Step 6 Replace N by $N - 1$.
   Step 7 If $N \neq 0$ go to Step 3. Otherwise stop.

By considering the case $N = 5$, comment on the correctness of this algorithm.

Following the instructions gives the results shown in the table.

N	5	4	3	2	1	0
X	1	2	6	42	1806	
P	2	3	7	43	1807	

The integers 2, 3, 7 and 43 are all prime. However, $1807 = 13 \times 139$, and is therefore not prime, so the algorithm is not correct.

Proving the correctness or otherwise of an algorithm can be extremely difficult. However, now that so much of international military and commercial affairs is dependent upon automated procedures carried out by computers, considerable effort has to be put into checking the correctness of these procedures and debugging (correcting) any which have flaws.

Working through the steps of an algorithm to check its correctness is sometimes called **tracing** the algorithm.

Another feature of algorithms illustrated by Example 1.4.1 is that of a stopping condition. As soon as $N = 0$ in Step 7, the procedure stops.

The algorithm in Example 1.4.2 has two stopping conditions. These occur in Step 2 and in Step 5.

Example 1.4.2
An algorithm is defined as follows.

> **Step 1** Read X.
> **Step 2** If $X < 0$ then stop.
> **Step 3** Let $A = 1$.
> **Step 4** Replace A by $\frac{1}{2}\left(A + \dfrac{X}{A}\right)$.
> **Step 5** If $\left| X - A^2 \right| < 0.001$, then stop.
> **Step 6** Go to Step 4.

(a) What is the purpose of this algorithm?
(b) What would happen if Step 2 were omitted?

> (a) For any inputted number X, the algorithm is attempting to find a number A such that $X - A^2$ is very small, that is, such that A is an approximation to $\sqrt{X}$.
>
> (b) A^2 can never be negative and so can never be very close to any value of X which is negative. The additional stopping condition of Step 2 is therefore necessary to make sure the procedure stops when the number X which is input is negative.

Example 1.4.2 also illustrates the idea of generality. Without Step 2, the algorithm in Example 1.4.2 would be correct for any positive value of X but would not be correct 'in general'. An important aspect of any algorithm is whether or not it is correct for all possible inputs or whether it is only correct for a certain range of inputs.

1.5 The Shell Sort algorithm

When either the Bubble Sort algorithm or the Shuttle Sort algorithm is applied to a set of n numbers, the number of comparisons can be as high as $1 + 2 + \ldots + (n-1) = \frac{1}{2}n(n-1)$. For small n, this number of comparisons can be made very quickly. However, for large n, an appreciably quicker method is the Shell Sort, named after D. L. Shell, who introduced this method in 1959. Shell's idea was to split a large set of numbers into smaller subsets, apply the Shuttle Sort algorithm to each subset and then gradually merge subsets together, using further applications of the Shuttle Sort algorithm as the subsets are merged.

To sort a list of n numbers, $A(1), A(2), \ldots, A(n)$:

Shell Sort

Step 1 Let $X = n$.

Step 2 Replace X by $\frac{1}{2}X$, ignoring any remainder.

Step 3 Apply the Shuttle Sort algorithm to each of the X sublists:

$$
\begin{array}{cccc}
A(1), & A(X+1), & A(2X+1), & \ldots \\
A(2), & A(X+2), & A(2X+2), & \ldots \\
\ldots & \ldots & \ldots & \ldots \\
\ldots & \ldots & \ldots & \ldots \\
A(X-1), & A(2X-1), & A(3X-1), & \ldots \\
A(X), & A(2X), & A(3X), & \ldots
\end{array}
$$

Step 4 If $X > 1$ then go to Step 2.

Step 5 Stop.

This complicated-looking algorithm will be illustrated with an example and a commentary.

Example 1.5.1

(a) Apply the Shell Sort algorithm to the list of numbers which are initially in reverse order:

   $9, 8, 7, 6, 5, 4, 3, 2, 1, 0.$

(b) Count the number of comparisons required for the list in part (a). How many comparisons would have been needed if the Shuttle Sort algorithm had initially been applied to the entire list?

(a) The first time Step 2 is performed, X, which was 10, becomes 5. So the 5 sublists to be sorted by Step 3 are:
   $A(1), A(6); \quad A(2), A(7); \quad A(3), A(8); \quad A(4), A(9); \quad A(5), A(10)$.

The working for Step 3 can then be laid out as shown below.

$$
\begin{array}{cccccccccc}
9 & 8 & 7 & 6 & 5 & 4 & 3 & 2 & 1 & 0 \\
9 & & & & & 4 & & & & \\
& 8 & & & & & 3 & & & \\
& & 7 & & & & & 2 & & \\
& & & 6 & & & & & 1 & \\
& & & & 5 & & & & & 0
\end{array}
$$

Sorting each pair then produces:

   $4 \quad 3 \quad 2 \quad 1 \quad 0 \quad 9 \quad 8 \quad 7 \quad 6 \quad 5$

The second time Step 2 is performed, X is made equal to 2 because $\frac{5}{2} = 2.5$, which, when you ignore the remainder, becomes 2. So the sublists to be sorted are
   $A(1), A(3), A(5), A(7), A(9) \quad$ and $\quad A(2), A(4), A(6), A(8), A(10)$,
where these numbers apply to the new list.

4	3	2	1	0	9	8	7	6	5
4		2		0		8		6	
	3		1		9		7		5

Sorting each subset of five elements then produces:

0	1	2	3	4	5	6	7	8	9

The third time Step 2 is performed, X is made equal to $\frac{2}{2} = 1$ and so the final pass of the Shuttle Sort algorithm takes place on the whole list, producing:

0	1	2	3	4	5	6	7	8	9

(b) The first time Step 3 was performed, the number of comparisons was 5, that is, 1 for each of the five sets.

The second time Step 3 was performed, the number of comparisons was:

4	2	0	0	0		3	1	1	1	1
2	4	2	2	2		1	3	3	3	3
0	0	4	4	4		9	9	9	7	5
8	8	8	8	6		7	7	7	9	7
6	6	6	6	8		5	5	5	5	9

Comparisons $1+2+1+2 = 6$ Comparisons $1+1+2+3 = 7$

The third and final time Step 3 was performed, the number of comparisons was 9. The total number was therefore $5+6+7+9 = 27$.

Applying the Shuttle Sort algorithm directly would have required $1+2+\ldots+9 = 45$ comparisons.

Note that the Shell Sort algorithm has produced a considerable saving in computing time even for a list with as few as 10 elements.

1.6   The Quicksort algorithm

You have seen that the Shell Sort algorithm is relatively fast compared with the Shuttle Sort algorithm for large values of n. Another sorting method which is similarly fast for large values of n is called the Quicksort algorithm. Like the Shell Sort algorithm, the Quicksort algorithm is based upon the idea of splitting the original list into sublists. However, it operates in the opposite fashion by gradually dealing with smaller and smaller sublists.

Quicksort

Step 1   Choose the number located in the middle of the list as the **pivot**, P.
{If the list has an even number of elements then choose either of the middle two numbers.}

Step 2   Go through the list putting any numbers less than P to the left of P, and any greater than P to the right. This creates two new sublists. {Note that the numbers in each sublist are kept in their original order.}

Step 3   If each sublist has just one element, then stop. Otherwise go to Step 2 for each sublist.

Note that although Step 1 tells you to choose the middle number as the pivot, in fact any number in the list could be chosen as the pivot. Choosing the middle number is best when the original list is already roughly in order but, otherwise, it can be simpler just to choose the first number in each list as the pivot.

Example 1.6.1
Use the Quicksort algorithm to rearrange the following numbers into ascending order, showing the new arrangement at each stage. Take the middle number in any list as the pivot.

$$12 \quad 3 \quad 20 \quad 15 \quad 1 \quad 25 \quad 17$$

The first step is to choose the pivot. This is the middle member of the list, and it is put into a box, for convenience.

$$12 \quad 3 \quad 20 \quad \boxed{15} \quad 1 \quad 25 \quad 17$$

Putting the elements less than the pivot on the left, and the others on the right gives the following list.

$$12 \quad 3 \quad 1 \quad \boxed{15} \quad 20 \quad 25 \quad 17$$

Looking at the sublist to the left of the pivot, the new pivot is 3. Arranging the sublist so that the terms which are less than 3 are to the left of it, and the terms which are greater to the right of it gives this new list.

$$1 \quad \boxed{3} \quad 12 \quad \boxed{15} \quad 20 \quad 25 \quad 17$$

Applying the same procedure to the sublist which is to the right of the pivot, the new pivot is 25, and the new list is

$$1 \quad \boxed{3} \quad 12 \quad \boxed{15} \quad 20 \quad 17 \quad \boxed{25}$$

There is still a sublist of two numbers, 20, 17 which needs to be sorted, so applying Step 2 with 20 as pivot gives

$$1 \quad \boxed{3} \quad 12 \quad \boxed{15} \quad 17 \quad \boxed{20} \quad 25$$

Each sublist now has one element, so the algorithm stops.

In practice, for large values of n and for randomly ordered initial lists, the Quicksort algorithm turns out to be the quickest of the algorithms you have met in this chapter – hence its name!

Exercise 1B

1 (a) Carry out the procedure of Example 1.4.1 in the case $N = \frac{1}{2}$. What happens?

 (b) Modify the algorithm to overcome the problem you noted in part (a).

2 Use the Shell Sort algorithm to rearrange the following numbers into ascending order. Show the new arrangement at each stage and count the number of comparisons required.

 3,   1,   8,   7,   5,   9,   2,   6.

3 (a) Use the Quicksort algorithm to rearrange the following colours into alphabetical order, showing the new arrangement at each stage. Take the first colour in any list as the pivot.

 Pink,   Black,   Red,   Green,   Orange,   White.

 (b) Find the maximum number of comparisons that could be needed to sort a list of six words into alphabetical order. Take the first word in any list as the pivot.

 (c) Find an expression for the maximum number of comparisons that could be needed to sort a list of n words into alphabetical order. (AQA)

4 (a) Use the Quicksort algorithm to rearrange the following numbers into order, showing the new arrangement at each stage. Take the first number in any list as the pivot.

 9,   5,   7,   11,   2,   8,   6,   17.

 (b) A Shuttle Sort algorithm is to be used to rearrange a list of numbers into order.

 (i) Find the maximum number of comparisons that would be needed to be certain that a list of eight numbers was in order.

 (ii) Find, in a simplified form, an expression for the maximum number of comparisons that would be needed to be certain that a list containing n numbers was in order. (AQA)

5 (a) Consider this algorithm which operates on N items: $A(1), A(2), \ldots, A(N)$.

 For $I = 2$ to N
 For $J = 0$ to $I - 2$
 If $A(I - J) < A(I - J - 1)$ then exchange $A(I - J)$ and $A(I - J - 1)$
 Next J
 Next I

 (i) Trace the algorithm in the case when $N = 4$ and the array contains

 $A(1) = 47$, $A(2) = 69$, $A(3) = 8$, $A(4) = 52$.

 (ii) Write down the name of this algorithm.

 (b) Use the Shell Sort algorithm to sort the list {4, 10, 3, 7, 2, 1, 8, 11, 7, 12}, indicating where it uses the algorithm specified in part (a), the output of which may be written down directly each time it is used. (AQA, adapted)

1.7 Flow diagrams

A flow diagram is a pictorial representation of an algorithm. Differently shaped boxes are used for different types of instruction. Fig. 1.6 shows you which instructions go into which boxes.

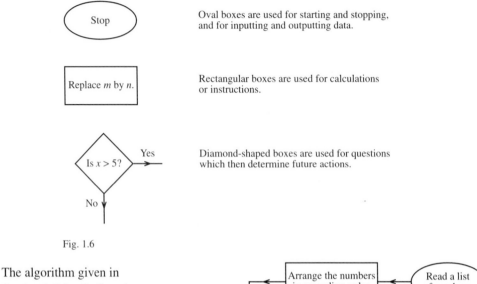

Oval boxes are used for starting and stopping, and for inputting and outputting data.

Rectangular boxes are used for calculations or instructions.

Diamond-shaped boxes are used for questions which then determine future actions.

Fig. 1.6

The algorithm given in Section 1.2 for finding the median of a set of numbers can be represented by the flow diagram in Fig. 1.7.

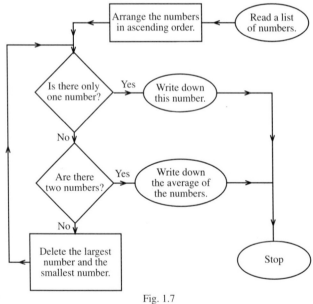

Fig. 1.7

1.8 Notation for algorithms

In Fig. 1.6, the rectangle contained the instruction 'Replace m by n'. Think of m and n as labels of pigeon-holes, each of them containing a number. This instruction means take the number which is in pigeon-hole n and put it into pigeon-hole m, replacing the number which is already there. The notation used in this book for this instruction will be $m = n$.

Similarly, $m = 2$ means put the number 2 into pigeon-hole m; and $m = m - 1$ means take the number already in pigeon-hole m, subtract 1 from it, and put the result back into pigeon-hole m.

These pigeon-holes are usually called **stores**.

Example 1.8.1
An algorithm has a flow diagram which is shown below.
(a) What is the output if $N = 57$?
(b) What has this algorithm been designed to do?

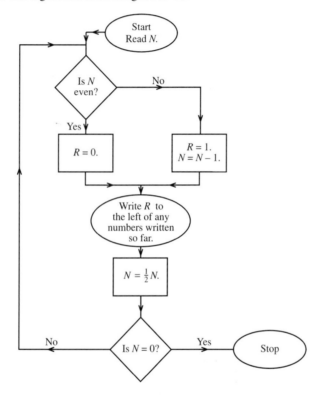

(a) After successive passes around the flow diagram, the values of N, R and the numbers written down so far are as shown in the table.

Pass	N	R	Written down
1	28	1	1
2	14	0	01
3	7	0	001
4	3	1	1001
5	1	1	11001
6	0	1	111001

(b) The algorithm converts N into a binary number. So, for example,

$$57 = (1 \times 32) + (1 \times 16) + (1 \times 8) + (0 \times 4) + (0 \times 2) + (1 \times 1) = 111001_2.$$

Sometimes when you see algorithms, you will see explanatory comments written about some or all of the steps. These will usually be put into curly brackets, {}, often called braces.

Here is an example of an algorithm with comments. It produces a permutation of the numbers 1 to n, that is, it produces the numbers 1 to n in random order, with no repeats. Notice how the comments make the algorithm easier to understand.

Step 1 Read n.   { n is the number of numbers in the permutation.}

Step 2 $i = 1$.   { i is the number of the permutation currently being found.}

Step 3 $r = Rand(1, n)$ { $Rand(1, n)$ is a random integer
                                                              between 1 and n inclusive.}

Step 4 If r has not already been used, write r, otherwise go to Step 3.
                                              { r is the ith number in the permutation.}

Step 5 $i = i + 1$.   {To get the next number in the permutation.}

Step 6 If $i < n$ go to Step 3, otherwise stop.

This algorithm is not very efficient, because you can spend much time regenerating random numbers which you have already found. You will find a much better algorithm in Miscellaneous exercise 1 Question 10.

Miscellaneous exercise 1

1 A flow diagram is shown below.

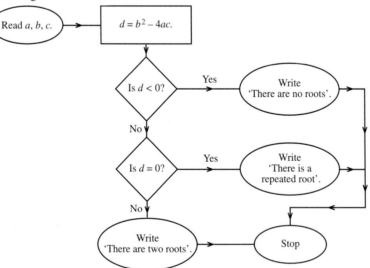

(a) What is the output of this algorithm in the cases
   (i) $a = 1$, $b = 3$, $c = 2$;   (ii) $a = 1$, $b = 2$, $c = 1$;   (iii) $a = 1$, $b = 2$, $c = 3$?
(b) What has this algorithm been designed to do?
(c) How could you adapt the flow diagram to represent an algorithm to find the roots of a quadratic equation?

2 (a) Carry out the algorithm in this flow diagram for $x = 2$, $x = 3$ and $x = 5$.

(b) For what is this algorithm designed?

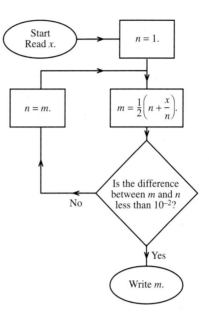

3 Euclid's algorithm is defined as follows.

Step 1 Read X and Y.

Step 2 If $X = Y$ then print X and stop.

Step 3 Replace the larger of X and Y by the difference between X and Y.

Step 4 Go back to Step 2.

(a) Carry out Euclid's algorithm for inputs of

  (i) 6 and 15,   (ii) 4 and 18,   (iii) 3 and 7.

(b) What does Euclid's algorithm find?

(c) Draw a flow diagram for this algorithm.

4 The Russian peasant's algorithm is defined as shown in the diagram.

Complete a table showing the successive values of x, y and t, when x and y initially take the values 11 and 9. Hence decide what the algorithm is designed to do.

5 An algorithm to sort a list, L, of numbers into increasing order is defined as follows.

Step 1 Write down the first number of L as the start of a new list N.

Step 2 Take the next number of L. Compare it to each number of N in turn (from the left) and insert it at the appropriate place in N.

Step 3 Repeat Step 2 until all numbers of L have been placed in N.

Note that for each number from L, once you have found a number in N that is bigger than it, you do not need to make any further comparisons.

(a) Use this algorithm to sort $L = \{8, 12, 2, 54, 23, 31\}$. Write down the list N and count the number of comparisons at each stage.

(b) Order the list L in such a way that the algorithm will require the largest possible number of comparisons.

(c) What is the largest possible number of comparisons needed for this algorithm to sort a list of n numbers?

6 The following algorithm is based on a method used by Archimedes to estimate π.

Step 1 $C = \frac{1}{2}\sqrt{3}$, $S = 3$, $T = 2\sqrt{3}$, $D = 2\sqrt{3} - 3$.

Step 2 Repeat
$$C = \sqrt{\tfrac{1}{2}(1 + C)}.$$
$$S = \frac{S}{C}.$$
$$T = \frac{S}{C}.$$
$$D = T - S.$$
Until $D < 0.01$.

Step 3 Print S.

(a) Copy and complete the following table to show the values of C, S, T and D (rounded to 4 decimal places) for the first three runs through the repeat loop.

	C	S	T	D
Initial values	0.8660	3.0000	3.4641	0.4641
1st iteration	0.9659	3.1058	3.2154	0.1096
2nd iteration				
3rd iteration				

(b) Write down the number of runs through the repeat loop that are needed if the value 0.01 (in line 7 of the algorithm) is replaced by 0.1.

(c) Let d_n be the value of D from the nth iteration. Use the values of d_1, d_2 and d_3 to conjecture an approximate value for $\dfrac{d_{n+1}}{d_n}$.

(d) Hence suggest an approximate expression for the value of D from the nth iteration.

(OCR, adapted)

7 The following algorithm has been written to input a set of 30 examination marks, each expressed as an integer percentage, find the minimum mark and output the result.

Line

1   SET MIN = 100

2   FOR $I = 1$ to 30

3   INPUT MARK

4   IF MARK < MIN

5   THEN MIN = MARK

6   NEXT N

7   ....

(a) (i)   State the purpose of Line 1 of the algorithm.

(ii)   There is a mistake in Line 6. Write down a corrected version of this line.

(iii)   The contents of Line 7 are missing. Write down the contents of Line 7 to ensure that the algorithm is fully complete.

(b) Show how this algorithm could be adapted if the number of examination marks to be input was unknown.

(c) Write an algorithm that would input a set of 50 examination marks, each expressed as an integer percentage, find the maximum mark and output the result.   (AQA)

8 A student is writing a computer program to calculate part of a multiplication table. This is the algorithm she uses.

$X = 0, K = 0$

FOR $I = 1$ TO 6

FOR $J = 1$ TO 5

$X = I \times J$

$K = K + 1$

PRINT K, I, "times", J, "equals", X

NEXT J

NEXT I

END

(a) State

(i)   the purpose of the line $X = 0, K = 0$,

(ii)   why the lines NEXT J, NEXT I are given in that order,

(iii)   the purpose of the variable K.

(b) When the value of K printed is 8, find the corresponding printed values of I, J and X.

(AQA)

9 The Binary Search algorithm described below locates the position of a certain value, X, within an ordered sequence $S(1)$, $S(2)$, ..., $S(N)$.

INT$(0.5(I + J))$ gives the largest integer that is less than or equal to $0.5(I + J)$.

Step 1 $I = 1$, $J = N$.   { I and J mark the boundaries of the sequence being searched.}

Step 2   If $I > J$ then print 'FAIL' and stop.   { X has not been found.}

Step 3 $M = \text{INT}(0.5(I + J))$.

Step 4   If $X = S(M)$ then print M and stop.   { X has been found.}

Step 5   If $X < S(M)$ then $J = M - 1$, otherwise $I = M + 1$.   {Reset boundaries.}

Step 6   Go to Step 2.

(a) Demonstrate carefully each step of the algorithm when it is applied to the sequence

     1   1   2   3   5   8   13   21

(i)   with $X = 13$;

(ii) with $X = 15$.

If N is a power of 2, the length of the sequence to be searched is at least halved at each iteration.

(b) If $N = 10$, work out the maximum possible length of the sequence to be searched at each iteration.

10* This algorithm produces a random permutation of the numbers from 1 to n; that is, it produces the numbers from 1 to n in random order, with no repeats.

Step 1   Read n.   { n is the number of numbers in the permutation.}

Step 2   For $i = 1$ to n, $Perm(i) = i$.   { $Perm(i)$ will be the ith number in the permutation. This is an initialisation step.}

Step 3 $j = 1$.

Step 4   Repeat the following.

     $r = Rand(j, n)$.   { $Rand(j, n)$ is a random number from j to n inclusive.}

     Swap $Perm(j)$ with $Perm(r)$,

     $j = j + 1$.

    Until $j = n - 1$.

Step 5   Write $Perm(1)$, $Perm(2)$, ..., $Perm(n)$.

(a) Work through the algorithm with $n = 5$, in the case when the random numbers produced are successively, 3, 4, 3 and 5. What permutation do you finish with?

(b) How many times do you have to use the random number generator when there are n numbers?

(c) Compare this with the algorithm on page 14.

2 Graphs and networks

This chapter looks at problems which can be represented using graphs and networks. When you have completed it you should

- know what is meant by the terms 'edge', 'vertex, 'trail', 'path', 'tree', 'cycle', 'directed' and 'planar', as applied to graphs
- be able to use the orders of the vertices of a graph to determine if the graph is Eulerian or semi-Eulerian
- be familiar with some special graphs, namely complete graphs, bipartite graphs, trees and digraphs
- know that $V = E + 1$ for any tree.

2.1 Graphs and networks

Fig. 2.1 LRT Registered User No 00/3261.

The standard London Underground map, the central part of which is shown in Fig. 2.1, shows how the various stations are connected. It does not attempt to show other properties, such as distances, or whether or not the track is above or below ground.

A simple way to model connectedness is with a
graph, which consists of **vertices** (or **nodes**)
joined by **edges** (or **arcs**). The graph shown in
Fig. 2.2 has five vertices (the blobs) joined by
four edges.

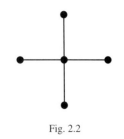

Fig. 2.2

Note this quite different use of the word 'graph'
from the conventional one.

The graph in Fig. 2.2 might represent one underground station which is linked directly
to four other stations. It could just as easily represent the methane molecule CH_4, or a
web site with five pages, one of which has links to the other four. In each case the graph
serves as a model highlighting the connectedness of the original real-world situation.

Graphs are allowed to have **loops**, connecting
vertices to themselves, as in Fig. 2.3a. They
may also have **multiple edges** between pairs of
vertices, as in Fig. 2.3b.

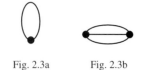

Fig. 2.3a   Fig. 2.3b

However, in many contexts loops and multiple edges are not appropriate. A graph
without loops and multiple edges is called a **simple** graph.

Fig. 2.4 shows all the simple graphs with 1, 2 and 3 vertices. There is one with 1 vertex,
two with 2 vertices and eight with 3 vertices.

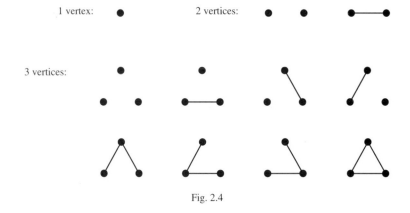

Fig. 2.4

All eleven of the graphs in Fig. 2.4 can be
thought of as being contained in the final one,
with 3 vertices and 3 edges. In graph-theory
terms you can say that each of them is a
subgraph of the graph shown in Fig. 2.5.

Fig. 2.5

A graph in which each of the vertices is connected by precisely one edge to every other vertex is called a **complete graph**. The notation K_n is used for the complete graph with n vertices. Fig. 2.6 shows K_2, K_3 and K_4.

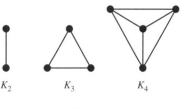

K_2 K_3 K_4

Fig. 2.6

Each simple graph is a subgraph of K_n for any sufficiently large n.

Example 2.1.1

Find a formula for the number of edges in the complete graph K_n.

Each vertex is connected to the other $n-1$ vertices and so it is at the end of $n-1$ edges. There are n vertices and so there are $n \times (n-1)$ ends of edges. As every edge has two ends, there are $\frac{1}{2}n(n-1)$ edges in total.

As a check, you can see that K_3 has $\frac{1}{2} \times 3 \times 2 = 3$ edges, and K_4 has $\frac{1}{2} \times 4 \times 3 = 6$ edges.

In addition to complete graphs, there is another important family of graphs, called **bipartite graphs**. Bipartite graphs have two sets of vertices. The edges only connect vertices from one set to the other, and do not connect vertices within a set. Fig. 2.7 shows a bipartite graph, with a set of 2 vertices in one oval, and a set of 3 vertices in another oval.

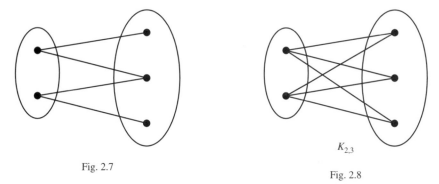

$K_{2,3}$

Fig. 2.7

Fig. 2.8

Note that it is not necessary for every vertex in one set to be connected to every vertex in the other.

If, in a bipartite graph, every vertex in one set is connected to every vertex in the other set, the graph is called a **complete bipartite graph**. If there are r vertices in one set, and s vertices in the other, the complete bipartite graph is denoted by $K_{r,s}$. Fig. 2.8 shows $K_{2,3}$.

2.2   Leonhard Euler

Leonhard Euler was an 18th-century Swiss mathematician who made major contributions to an enormous range of aspects of pure and applied mathematics, physics, and astronomy. Much of the notation he used, including the symbols e and π, has remained in standard use to the present day.

Euler is known as the father of graph theory. One
of his main contributions is reputed to have arisen
from a puzzle about the seven bridges over the
river Pregel in the Prussian city of Königsberg,
shown in Fig. 2.9. Can you find a 'circular' tour
which crosses each bridge precisely once?

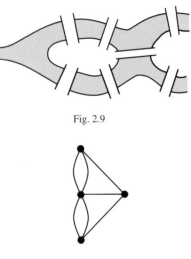

Fig. 2.9

A suitable graphical representation of the
Königsberg Bridge problem has the four land-masses
represented by vertices and the bridges represented by
edges, as in Fig. 2.10.

Euler realised that, in any circular tour, a land-mass is
entered (via a bridge) the same number of times as it is
left (via a bridge). For a circular tour to exist, each
land-mass would therefore need to be linked to the
other land-masses by an even number of bridges. So a

Fig. 2.10

circular tour would require each vertex of Fig. 2.10 to have an even number of edges coming
out of it. In fact, the numbers of edges are 3, 3, 3 and 5, and so a circular tour is impossible.

A few definitions of graph theory terms are needed to move forward. These definitions
will be illustrated with reference to the section of the Underground map shown in
Fig. 2.11. You should regard *each* station as a vertex, not just the interchange stations.

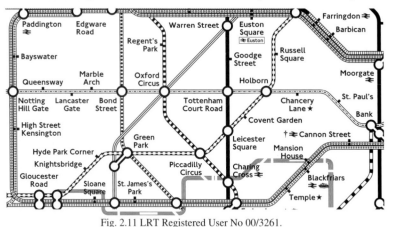

Fig. 2.11 LRT Registered User No 00/3261.

A **trail** is a sequence of edges such that the end vertex of one edge is the start vertex of
the next. One example is Green Park–Piccadilly Circus–Leicester Square–Charing
Cross–Piccadilly Circus–Oxford Circus–Bond Street.

A **path** is a trail with the restriction that no vertex is passed more than once. The trail
given above, which starts at Green Park, is therefore not a path, because Piccadilly
Circus occurs twice.

A **closed** trail is one where the initial and final vertices are the same. One example is Green Park–Piccadilly Circus–Leicester Square–Charing Cross–Piccadilly Circus–Green Park.

A **cycle** is a closed trail where only the initial and final vertices are the same. The closed trail given above is not a cycle itself but it contains the cycle, Piccadilly Circus–Leicester Square–Charing Cross–Piccadilly Circus. Although one vertex is allowed to be used twice, at the beginning and the end, no edge is allowed to be used twice.

The **order** of a vertex is the number of edges meeting at that vertex. For example, Oxford Circus has order 6, Temple has order 2 and Holborn has order 4. If the number of edges is even, the vertex has **even order**; if the number of edges is odd, the vertex has **odd order**. The order of a vertex is sometimes called its **degree**.

A **connected** graph is one where, for any two vertices, a path can be found connecting the two vertices.

2.3   Eulerian graphs

An **Eulerian graph** is a connected graph which has a closed trail containing every edge precisely once. Fig. 2.12 contains one Eulerian graph, and one graph which is not Eulerian.

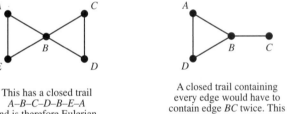

This has a closed trail
A–B–C–D–B–E–A
and is therefore Eulerian.

A closed trail containing
every edge would have to
contain edge *BC* twice. This
graph is therefore not Eulerian.

Fig. 2.12

It is a relatively easy task (see Exercise 2A Question 2) to prove that every vertex of an Eulerian graph must have even order.

Euler proved both this result and its converse (which is much more difficult to prove).

A connected graph is Eulerian if and only if every vertex has even order.

Example 2.3.1

(a) Explain why the graph in Fig. 2.13 is not Eulerian.

(b) Which single edge could be deleted in order to make the resultant graph Eulerian? Explain your answer and find a closed trail containing all the remaining edges.

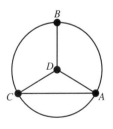

(a) Vertices *B* and *D* have odd order.

Fig. 2.13

(b) Removing edge *BD* creates a connected graph with every vertex having even order. This is therefore Eulerian. An example of a closed trail is *ABCACDA*.

A well known modern puzzle is to trace the diagram shown in Fig. 2.14 without lifting the pen off the paper and without going over any lines twice.

In graph theory terms the problem is therefore to find a trail (not necessarily closed) which contains every edge precisely once. The initial and final vertices, if different, will then have odd order, whereas all other vertices will have even order.

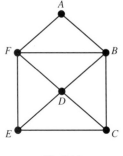

Fig. 2.14

In Fig. 2.14, only vertices *C* and *E* have odd order and therefore the trick is to make sure you start tracing from one or other of these two points. An example, is *CBAFBDCEDFE*.

A graph is called **semi-Eulerian** if it has a trail which is not closed that contains every edge precisely once.

> A connected graph is semi-Eulerian if and only if precisely two vertices have odd order.

Exercise 2A

1 Which of the following graphs are Eulerian and which are semi-Eulerian?

(a)   (b)   (c)   (d)

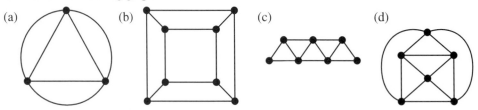

2 Explain carefully why an Eulerian graph can only have vertices of even order.

3 Draw connected graphs which have

    (a) 1 vertex of order 1 and 3 vertices of order 3,

    (b) 3 vertices of order 1 and 1 vertex of order 3.

4 Is it possible to find a route which passes through every door precisely once?

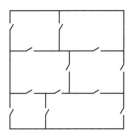

5 Think of one or two practical situations which it would be appropriate to model with a graph with multiple edges.

6 (a) What is the order of a vertex of K_n?

　(b) For what value of n is K_n Eulerian or semi-Eulerian?

7 (a) How many edges are there in the complete bipartite graph $K_{r,s}$?

　(b) Analyse $K_{r,s}$ in terms of being Eulerian or semi-Eulerian.

8 Four Members of Parliament, Ann, Brian, Clare and David, are being considered for four cabinet posts. Ann could be Foreign Secretary or Home Secretary, Brian could be Home Secretary or the Chancellor of the Exchequer, Clare could be Foreign Secretary or the Minister for Education and David could be the Chancellor or the Home Secretary.

　(a) Draw a bipartite graph to represent this situation.

　(b) How many options does the Prime Minister have?

2.4 Trees

A tree is a connected graph with no cycles. All of the graphs in Fig. 2.15 are trees.

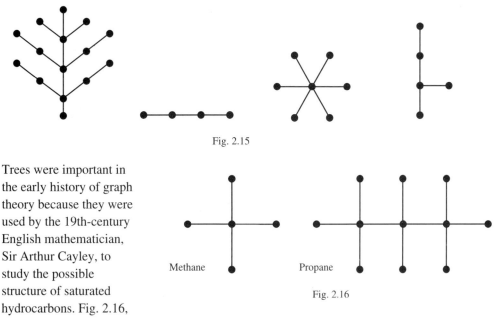

Fig. 2.15

Trees were important in the early history of graph theory because they were used by the 19th-century English mathematician, Sir Arthur Cayley, to study the possible structure of saturated hydrocarbons. Fig. 2.16,

Methane　　　　Propane

Fig. 2.16

in which vertices of order 4 represent carbon atoms and vertices of order 1 represent hydrogen atoms, shows methane, CH_4, and propane, C_3H_8.

Trees are also important in the study of connected graphs. Any connected graph contains at least one subgraph which is a tree connecting every vertex of the original graph. The complete graph K_4 has many such trees. Fig. 2.17 shows just one example obtained by removing successive edges.

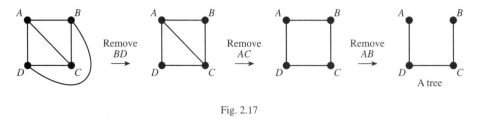

Fig. 2.17

Example 2.4.1

Complete a table for the number of vertices and edges in each of the trees of Fig. 2.15. What do you notice?

V	15	4	7	5
E	14	3	6	6

You can see from the table that $V = E + 1$.

The result $V = E + 1$ is actually true for *all* trees and is a special case of a result which Leonhard Euler proved for all connected **planar** graphs, that is, graphs which can be drawn in a plane in such a way that edges only meet at vertices.

Note that the graph shown in Fig. 2.18a is planar because it can be drawn as shown in Fig. 2.18b.

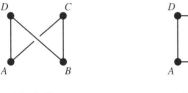

Fig. 2.18a   Fig. 2.18b

What Euler noticed, and then proved, was that if a connected graph, drawn in a plane, had R regions, V vertices and E edges, then

$$R + V = E + 2.$$

In the case of Fig. 2.18b, $R = 2$, $V = 4$ and $E = 4$ and so $R + V = 6 = E + 2$, as expected.

A tree has no cycles and so $R = 1$ for any tree. Then, substituting $R = 1$ in Euler's relationship $R + V = E + 2$ gives $1 + V = E + 2$, which reduces to $V = E + 1$.

> For any graph drawn in a plane, Euler's relationship is $R + V = E + 2$.
>
> For any tree, $R = 1$ and $V = E + 1$.

2.5 Network problems

For many problems, you need to know more than just whether vertices are connected or not. For example, problems involving the distance between towns or the costs of various links require a numerical value to be given to each edge. Such a numerical value is given the general title of a **weight**. A graph whose edges have weights can be called either a 'weighted graph' or a **network**.

A simple network is shown in Fig. 2.19.

Most of the remainder of this book is concerned with problems about networks. You might like to try to think of as many different types of questions as you can about the network in Fig. 2.19.

Here are some possibilities.

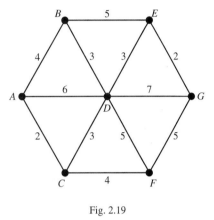

Fig. 2.19

- The connections of minimum weight which connect all of the vertices. This is called the minimum connector problem; see Chapter 3.
- The route of minimum weight from A to G. This is the shortest path problem; see Chapter 4.
- The closed trail of minimum weight which includes every edge at least once. This is the route inspection problem; see Chapter 6.
- The cycle of minimum weight which includes every vertex. This is the travelling salesperson problem; see Chapter 7.

2.6 Directed graphs

Sometimes the links which are represented by edges have a direction associated with them. For example, some roads are one-way, and a page on one company's web site may have a link to that of an advertiser but without there being any reciprocal link.

A graph with directed edges is known as a directed graph, or **digraph**.

Fig. 2.20

In Fig. 2.20, the digraph has three directed edges, and two edges which can be traced in either direction.

Example 2.6.1

(a) Show that the digraph of Fig. 2.21 is Eulerian by finding all the closed trails which contain every directed edge.

(b) At each vertex of this Eulerian digraph, what is true about the number of edges in and the number of edges out?

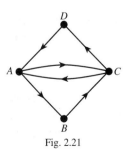

Fig. 2.21

(a) *ABCDACA*, *ABCACDA*

(b) At A, number of edges in = number of edges out = 2.
At B, number of edges in = number of edges out = 1.
At C, number of edges in = number of edges out = 2.
At D, number of edges in = number of edges out = 1.

The number of edges in is equal to the number of edges out, at every vertex.

2.7   Representing networks by matrices

It is important to have a way of representing networks which does not rely on a diagram. In particular, computers cannot work with diagrams, so how can you tell a computer all the essential detail about a network?

The answer is surprisingly simple. A table showing all the information about the weights in a network is all that you need. A table of this type is called a **matrix**.

For example, you can summarise the information
in Fig. 2.22 in the matrix

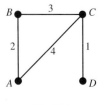

$$\begin{array}{c} \\ A \\ B \\ C \\ D \end{array} \begin{array}{cccc} A & B & C & D \\ \left(\begin{array}{cccc} - & 2 & 4 & - \\ 2 & - & 3 & - \\ 4 & 3 & - & 1 \\ - & - & 1 & - \end{array}\right) \end{array}.$$

Fig. 2.22

Notice that for a network in which all the links are two-way links, the matrix is symmetrical about the diagonal line drawn from the top left to the bottom right of the matrix. This diagonal is called the main diagonal of the matrix.

You can also store the information about weights in a digraph using a similar method, but the resulting matrix is no longer symmetrical about the main diagonal.

For example, you can summarise the information
in Fig. 2.23 in the matrix

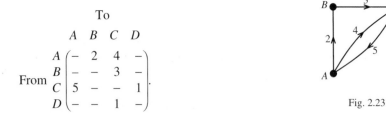

$$\text{To}$$
$$\text{From} \begin{array}{c} \\ A \\ B \\ C \\ D \end{array} \begin{array}{cccc} A & B & C & D \\ \left(\begin{array}{cccc} - & 2 & 4 & - \\ - & - & 3 & - \\ 5 & - & - & 1 \\ - & - & 1 & - \end{array}\right) \end{array}.$$

Fig. 2.23

As the matrix is no longer symmetrical it is important to make the directions of the links clear. If there is ambiguity the words 'From' and 'To' will be inserted to make it clear, for example, that the entry 5 means that there is an edge of weight 5 from C to A.

If you reconstruct the network from the matrix, you should realise that your reconstruction may appear very different from someone else's reconstruction. For example, the digraph in Fig. 2.24 gives rise to the same matrix as the digraph in Fig. 2.23.

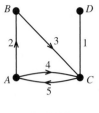

Fig. 2.24

Exercise 2B

1 (a) A network is used to represent the times taken to travel between various cities. Why might directed edges be appropriate?

   (b) What type of electrical networks are best represented by

   (i) digraphs,   (ii) undirected graphs?

2 Write down two matrices which represent the graph and the digraph shown in the figure.

3 For the network shown in the diagram,

   (a) find the connections of minimum weight which connect all the vertices;

   (b) find the route from A to G of minimum weight.

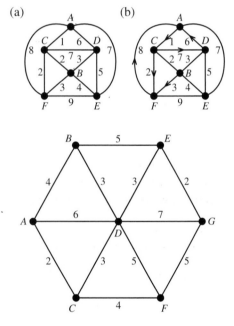

4 Draw several trees, with vertices of orders 1 or 4 only, to represent possible saturated hydrocarbons. What is the connection between the number of hydrogen atoms (vertices of order 1) and the number of carbon atoms (vertices of order 4)?

5 Design a flow diagram for an algorithm that deletes edges from any connected graph and produces a tree on the same vertices. (You must ensure that deleting an edge does not disconnect the graph.)

6 The 'even-weight code of length 3' uses four code-words, 000, 011, 101 and 110. The 'distance' between two of these code-words is the number of places in which the binary digits differ.

(a) Draw a network to illustrate the distances between the four code-words.

(b) When transmitting and receiving codes, what is the advantage of using code-words in which all distances are at least 2?

7 Suppose that at a social gathering the number of handshakes that occur is H. Suppose further that there are n people, who shake hands h_1, h_2, ... and h_n times respectively.

(a) What, in terms of H, is the sum of all the h_i?

(b) Represent people by vertices and handshakes by edges. What relationship does the result in part (a) imply about the orders of the vertices and the numbers of edges?

Miscellaneous exercise 2

1 Draw all the essentially different trees with 3, 4, 5 and 6 vertices.

2 (a) For the system of islands and bridges shown in the diagram, is it possible to find a trail which crosses every bridge precisely once? Carefully explain your reasoning.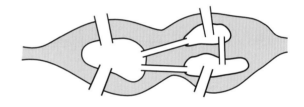

(b) Is it possible to find a closed trail with the same property?

3 (a) A, B, C and D are the vertices of the complete graph K_4. List all the paths (i.e. routes passing through particular vertices at most once) from A to B.

(b) How many paths are there from A to B in the complete graph on the vertices $\{A, B, C, D, E\}$?

(c) Which of the graphs in parts (a) and (b) are Euclidean, and why?

4 Show that the graph in the diagram is planar.   (AQA)

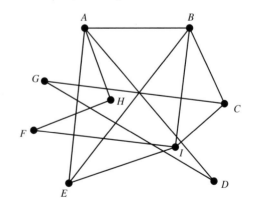

5 An algorithm for deciding whether a graph is planar or not is described below. (Note that it does not work for all graphs.)

Step 1 Find a cycle which passes through every vertex of the graph. If no such cycle can be found then report this fact and stop.

Step 2 Redraw the graph with this cycle drawn as a circle and with all edges not included in the cycle drawn as chords of the circle.

Step 3 Draw a new graph whose vertices represent the chords of the circle. Join two of these new vertices with an edge if the relevant chords cross each other.

Step 4 If the new graph is *not* bipartite then the original graph is non-planar. If the new graph *is* bipartite then the original graph is planar. Use the natural subdivision of the vertices of the bipartite graph to split the chords of Step 2 into two sets. Choose one of these sets of chords and redraw them as edges *outside* the circle.

Demonstrate the use of this algorithm by applying it to each of the following graphs. In each case show sufficient detail to make your working clear.

(a)   (b)   (c)

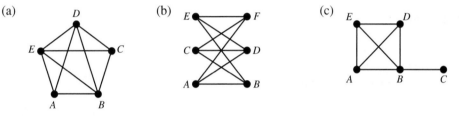

6 (a) A simple connected graph has 7 vertices, all having the same degree d. Give the possible values of d, and for each value of d give the number of edges of the graph.

(b) Another simple connected graph has 8 vertices, all having the same degree d. Draw such a graph with $d = 3$, and give the other possible values of d.   (AQA)

7 (a) G_1 is a simple connected graph with 4 vertices.

(i) What is the least number of edges that G_1 could have?

(ii) What is the greatest number of edges that G_1 could have?

(b) G_2 is a simple connected graph with n vertices.

(i) What is the least number of edges that G_2 could have?

(ii) What is the greatest number of edges that G_2 could have?   (AQA)

3 Minimum connector problems

This chapter looks at effective ways of connecting vertices of a network. When you have completed it you should

- know what a spanning tree for a connected graph is
- know the term 'greedy algorithm', and the steps of the greedy algorithms called Prim's and Kruskal's algorithms
- be able to find a spanning tree of minimum weight by using either Prim's algorithm or Kruskal's algorithm
- know that Prim's algorithm can easily be programmed for a computer, and be able to apply the algorithm in matrix form.

3.1 Introduction

To create an internal computer network in a school, cabling has to be laid between the five main computer areas. These five areas and the costs of the various alternative runs of cables are as shown in Fig. 3.1.

To connect all of the areas together just four runs of cable are needed. Three of the many possibilities are shown in Fig. 3.2.

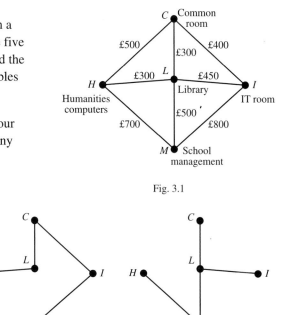

Fig. 3.1

Fig. 3.2

Find the costs of each one of these three possibilities. Can you find a cheaper way of laying the cable? (See Exercise 3A Question 3.)

You may well have been able to spot the solution to the simple problem posed above. However, for problems such as connecting cable TV to all the main areas of a town, linking up houses to the national electricity grid, or joining up soldering points on a printed circuit, the number of possible connections is so large that you have to use an algorithm that can be performed by a computer. The purpose of this chapter is to develop such an algorithm.

3.2   Spanning trees

You may have noticed that each of the possible runs of cable considered in Section 3.1 is a tree connecting together all of the vertices. Any tree which connects all the vertices of a graph is called a **spanning tree** for that graph.

Notice that each of the spanning trees contains the same number of edges, and that this number is one less than the number of vertices of the graph. This is illustrated in Fig. 3.3.

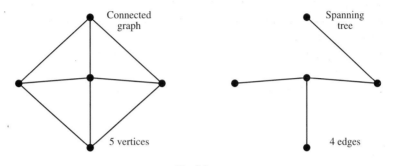

Fig. 3.3

This relationship between the number of vertices of the connected graph and the number of edges of the spanning tree is always true and is proved in Section 3.6.

For a connected graph with n vertices,
each spanning tree has precisely $n-1$ edges.

Example 3.2.1
Find the number of spanning trees of the graph in Fig. 3.4.

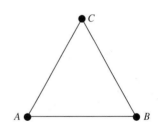

The graph has three vertices, so each spanning tree has two edges. There are three different ways of deleting an edge from the original graph, so the spanning trees are the three shown in Fig. 3.5.

Fig. 3.4

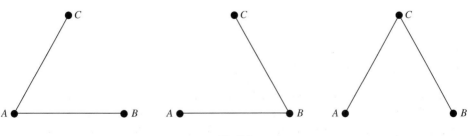

Fig. 3.5

Remember that a 'complete' graph is one which has every possible edge. The number of possible spanning trees for a complete graph increases very rapidly as the number of vertices increases (see Table 3.6).

Number of vertices	Number of spanning trees
3	3
4	16
...	...
20	2.6×10^{23}
...	...

Table 3.6

Fig. 3.7 shows the complete graph with four vertices. Fig. 3.8 shows the 16 possible spanning trees.

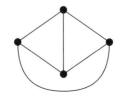

Fig. 3.7

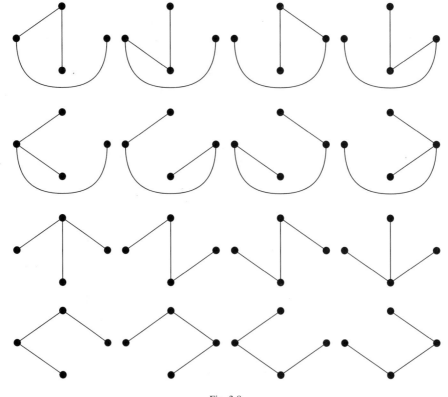

Fig. 3.8

For graphs with a reasonably large number of vertices, it is not possible for even the most powerful computer to scan all the possible spanning trees to find the best one for a problem like those in Section 3.1. To do it in a reasonable amount of time, you need an algorithm.

3.3   Prim's algorithm

The spanning tree of minimum weight is called the **minimum spanning tree**, or the **minimum connector**. For a given connected graph, Prim's algorithm is a quick method of finding the minimum spanning tree. The sequence of steps to be followed is shown below.

> **Prim's algorithm**   To find a minimum spanning tree T:
>
> **Step 1**   Select any vertex to be the first vertex of T.
>
> **Step 2**   Consider the edges which connect vertices in T to vertices outside T. Pick the one with minimum weight. Add this edge and the extra vertex to T. (If there are two or more edges of minimum weight, choose any one of them.)
>
> **Step 3**   Repeat Step 2 until T contains every vertex of the graph.

Example 3.3.1
Use Prim's algorithm to obtain a minimum spanning tree for the graph in Fig. 3.9.

The successive stages, starting with vertex C, are as shown in Fig. 3.10.

Notice that at the fourth stage, either FA or FB could have been chosen.

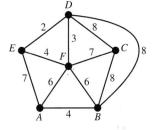

Fig. 3.9

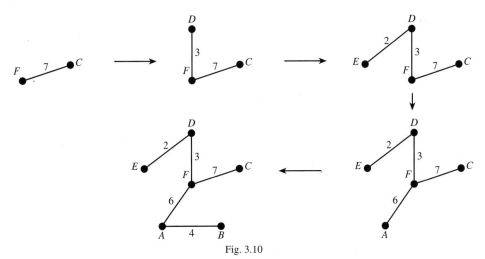

Fig. 3.10

The minimum spanning tree has weight $7 + 3 + 2 + 6 + 4 = 22$ units.

Notice that when you apply Prim's algorithm, you are simply choosing the edge which is immediately 'best' without being concerned about the long-term consequences of your choice. The fact that this 'greedy' approach to the minimum connector problem always leads to the best solution is justified in Section 3.6.

3.4 Kruskal's algorithm

One of several alternative algorithms for finding the minimum spanning tree uses edge weights directly rather than considering connecting up points. It was invented by an American mathematician, Martin Kruskal.

Kruskal's algorithm

To find a minimum spanning tree for a connected graph with n vertices:

Step 1 Choose the edge of least weight.

Step 2 Choose from those edges remaining the edge of least weight which does *not* form a cycle with already chosen edges. (If there are several such edges, choose one arbitrarily.)

Step 3 Repeat Step 2 until $n-1$ edges have been chosen.

Example 3.4.1

Apply Kruskal's algorithm to the network in Fig. 3.11.

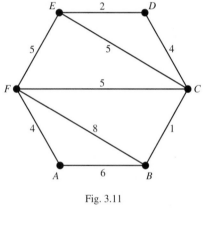

Fig. 3.11

Starting with the edge of least weight, which is BC, of weight 1, Kruskal's algorithm gives the results in Table 3.12.

Edge	Weight	Choice
BC	1	1st
DE	2	2nd
AF	4	3rd
CD	4	4th
CE	5	Not chosen
CF	5	5th
EF	5	–
AB	6	–
BF	8	–

Table 3.12

The resulting minimum spanning tree is shown in Fig. 3.13.

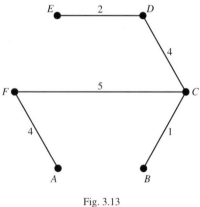

Fig. 3.13

Kruskal's algorithm is very easy to apply to a small network. The need to spot whether or not a cycle has been produced makes it less good for more involved questions and also less easy to program for a computer.

Exercise 3A

1 Find all the possible spanning trees for the
   graph in the figure.

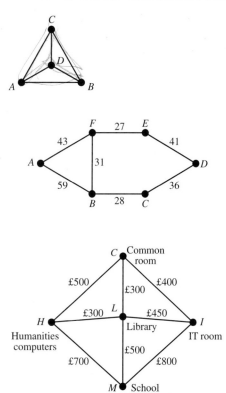

2 (a) Draw all possible spanning trees for
        this network.

   (b) Which of the spanning trees has
        minimum weight?

   (c) Use Prim's algorithm, starting with
        vertex A, to find the minimum
        spanning tree.

3 Find the cheapest way of laying the cable
   for the problem posed at the beginning of
   Section 3.1, whose diagram is reproduced
   here.

4 Consider the network of Question 2. Show that Kruskal's algorithm produces the same
   minimum spanning tree as Prim's algorithm.

5 Apply Kruskal's algorithm to the network
   shown here. Draw a diagram showing the
   minimum connector, state the order in
   which you added edges and work out the
   total length of the minimum connector.

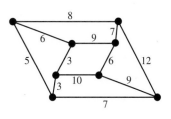

6 To obtain a minimum spanning tree, you can *delete* edges in order of decreasing weight.

   (a) When should an edge not be deleted?

   (b) Devise an algorithm for obtaining a minimum spanning tree by such a method of
        deletion.

3.5 Matrix formulation

Prim's algorithm can be translated relatively easily into a computer program. The best
starting point for this is the matrix which shows the weights on the various edges.

The graph used in Example 3.3.1 is tabulated in Table 3.14.

	A	B	C	D	E	F
A	–	4	–	–	7	6
B	4	–	8	8	–	6
C	–	8	–	8	–	7
D	–	8	8	–	2	3
E	7	–	–	2	–	4
F	6	6	7	3	4	–

Table 3.14

The solution to Example 3.3.1 would then proceed as follows.

Select vertex C to be the first vertex of T. Circle C in the top row to show that you have selected it, and cross out the C row.

Look for the smallest weight in the columns of the vertices in T (that is, the C column) and circle it. This is a 7, in row F. So F becomes the second vertex of the spanning tree. Select F by circling it in the top row, and cross out the F row. This gives Table 3.15.

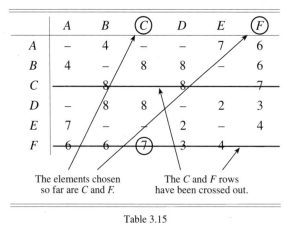

The elements chosen   The C and F rows
so far are C and F.   have been crossed out.

Table 3.15

Now circle the smallest weight in the columns corresponding to the vertices of T (that is, the C and F columns). This weight is 3, in row D, so choose D to be the third vertex of T: circle the D in the top row, and cross out the D row, as shown in Table 3.16.

	A	B	Ⓒ	Ⓓ	E	Ⓕ
A	–	4	–	–	7	6
B	4	–	8	8	–	6
C	—	8	—	8	—	7
D	—	8	8	—	2	③
E	7	–	–	2	–	4
F	6	6	⑦	3	4	—

Table 3.16

You can continue this procedure, successively choosing E, A and B. The final state of the matrix is shown in Table 3.17. The circled numbers give you the minimum spanning tree as found in Example 3.3.1.

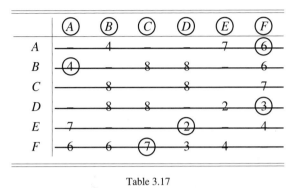

Table 3.17

The matrix formulation of Prim's algorithm to find a minimum spanning tree T is:

Step 1 Select any vertex to be the first vertex of T.

Step 2 Circle the new vertex of T in the top row, and cross out the row corresponding to this new vertex.

Step 3 Find the smallest weight left in the columns corresponding to the vertices of T, and circle this weight. Then choose the vertex whose row the weight is in to join T. (If there are several possibilities for the weight, choose any one of them.)

Step 4 Repeat Steps 2 and 3 until T contains every vertex.

Example 3.5.1

Find a minimum spanning tree for the weighted graph with the following matrix form.

	A	B	C	D	E	F	G	H
A	–	23	17	–	18	–	15	–
B	23	–	9	10	12	16	–	14
C	17	9	–	9	20	–	27	–
D	–	10	9	–	–	–	–	16
E	18	12	20	–	–	7	20	–
F	–	16	–	–	7	–	24	17
G	15	–	27	–	20	24	–	–
H	–	14	–	16	–	17	–	–

Select A as the first vertex of T. Circle A in the top row and cross out the A row.

Circle the smallest weight in the A column, which is 15. This corresponds to G, which becomes the next vertex of T. Circle G in the top row and cross out the G row.

The smallest remaining weight in the columns for vertices of T is 17, corresponding to C. Circle the 17, and C in the top row, and cross out the C row. At this stage the situation is:

	Ⓐ	B	Ⓒ	D	E	F	Ⓖ	H
A	—	23	17	—	18	—	15	—
B	23	–	9	10	12	16	–	14
C	(17)	9	—	9	20	—	27	—
D	–	10	9	–	–	–	–	16
E	18	12	20	–	–	7	20	–
F	–	16	–	–	7	–	24	17
G	(15)	—	27	—	20	24	—	—
H	–	14	–	16	–	17	–	–

Either of the two 9s in the C column could now be chosen. Arbitrarily, choose D to be the next vertex of T. Circle the 9, and the D in the top row, and cross out the D row.

Continue this process. You can carry out all the working in a single table:

Order of selection		Ⓐ	Ⓑ	Ⓒ	Ⓓ	Ⓔ	Ⓕ	Ⓖ	Ⓗ
1	A	—	23	17	—	18	—	15	—
5	B	23	—	(9)	10	12	16	—	14
3	C	(17)	9	—	9	20	—	27	—
4	D	—	10	(9)	—	—	—	—	16
6	E	18	(12)	20	—	—	7	20	—
7	F	—	16	—	—	(7)	—	24	17
2	G	(15)	—	27	—	20	24	—	—
8	H	—	(14)	—	16	—	17	—	—

The minimum spanning tree is illustrated in Fig. 3.18.

The minimum weight is
$15 + 17 + 9 + 9 + 12 + 14 + 7 = 83$
units.

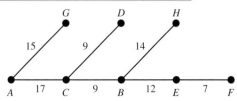

Fig. 3.18

Exercise 3B

1 The road distances in kilometres between eight towns are shown in the table. Boxes with thick borders refer to motorway routes.

	A	B	C	D	E	F	G	H
A	–	20	45	50	60	50	40	50
B	20	–	50	60	50	65	30	30
C	45	50	–	30	10	80	80	75
D	50	60	30	–	55	70	85	100
E	60	50	10	55	–	85	75	55
F	50	65	80	70	85	–	70	100
G	40	30	80	85	75	70	–	45
H	50	30	75	100	55	100	45	–

(a) Use Prim's algorithm, starting with A, to find the minimum connector for the towns. Draw a diagram showing the minimum connector, state the order in which you added edges, and work out the total length of the minimum connector.

(b) The time for journeys can be estimated by assuming an average speed of 100 km h^{-1} for the motorway routes and 60 km h^{-1} for the other roads. Complete a table of times, in minutes, between the towns. Find the minimum connector for the times, and write down the total of all the times on the minimum connector.

(c) Explain why the answer for part (b) is not the total time for the minimum connector found in part (a).

2 The costs in £ sterling of tickets for direct flights between six cities are shown in the table.

	A	B	C	D	E	F
A	–	45	60	50	90	145
B	45	–	70	25	80	110
C	60	70	–	55	70	320
D	50	25	55	–	35	175
E	90	80	70	35	–	80
F	145	110	320	175	80	–

(a) Use Prim's algorithm to construct a minimum connector. Show all your working clearly and state the order in which you add edges or vertices.

(b) Suppose that, in addition to the cost of tickets, an airport tax of 10% must be paid on leaving any airport. What effect will this have on the minimum connector?

(c) Suppose that airport taxes are actually £15 for any flight involving airports D, E or F and £5 otherwise. Work out the new minimum connector.

3 The figure shows the distances in kilometres along recommended motoring routes between ten French towns.

Dijon

296	Grenoble								
462	714	Le Mans							
507	282	926	Marseille						
662	334	1081	188	Nice					
297	549	138	761	916	Orléans				
313	565	203	776	931	130	Paris			
515	560	182	733	888	212	330	Poitiers		
244	139	507	309	464	392	513	421	St-Etienne	
415	534	82	745	900	112	234	100	425	Tours

(a) Use Prim's algorithm, starting with Paris, to find the minimum connector. Show all your working clearly, and work out the minimum connector's total length.

(b) The distances from Geneva (in Switzerland) to the ten French towns are as follows.

D	G	L	M	N	O	Pa	Po	S	T
199	144	634	434	477	496	537	501	164	528

What is the total length of the minimum connector when Geneva is included?

3.6* Justification of Prim's algorithm

The aim of this section is to show that, for any connected graph, Prim's algorithm in the form given in Section 3.3 will always produce a spanning tree of minimum possible weight. You may omit this section and assume the result if you wish.

Consider the formulation of Prim's algorithm given in Section 3.3.

> To find a minimum spanning tree T:
>
> **Step 1** Select any vertex to be the first vertex of T.
>
> **Step 2** Consider the edges which connect vertices in T to vertices outside T. Pick the one with minimum weight. Add this edge and the extra vertex to T. (If there are two or more edges of minimum weight, choose any one of them.)
>
> **Step 3** Repeat Step 2 until T contains every vertex of the graph.

In the justification, the following notation is used: T is formed by successively adding vertices $v_1, v_2, \ldots, v_n$ and edges $a_1, a_2, \ldots, a_{n-1}$.

The justification requires three results along the way. The first task is to prove that Prim's algorithm does always produce a spanning tree.

Result 1   For a connected graph G with n vertices, Prim's algorithm produces a subgraph T which
(a) has $n-1$ edges and n vertices,
(b) is connected,
(c) has no cycles,
(d) is a spanning tree.

 Justification

 (a) For Step 2 to be no longer possible, there would have to be no connections between vertices of T and any vertices not in T. Provided the original graph is connected, Step 2 can therefore always be repeated until T contains every vertex.

 Therefore T has n vertices. Starting from the initial vertex of T, each application of Step 2 adds one edge and one vertex to T. The number of edges of T is therefore one less than the number of vertices, which is $n-1$.

This completes the justification of (a).

Denote by T_i the graph formed by the addition of the vertex v_i.

 (b) By Step 1, T_1 consists simply of the vertex v_1. By Step 2, vertex v_2 is joined to T_1 by edge a_1, so T_2 is connected.

 Using Step 2 again, vertex v_3 is joined to T_2 by edge a_2. T_2 is connected, so there must be a route from v_3 to any vertex in T_2. So T_3 is also connected.

 Repeat this argument until all the vertices have been added. The final stage shows that T_n is connected. But $T_n = T$, so T is connected.

 (c) Suppose T has a cycle. Then let v_k be the vertex in this cycle with maximum possible k. In the cycle, v_k is joined by two edges to other vertices. These vertices must be in T_{k-1}, because of the maximality of k. However, by the definition of Prim's algorithm, v_k is only joined by a single edge to vertices of T_{k-1}. This is a contradiction, so T has no cycles.

 (d) From part (b), T is connected. It also has no cycles, by (c), and is therefore a tree. By (a) it spans G, because it has the same number of vertices as G, and it is therefore a spanning tree.

Result 1 shows that a spanning tree with n vertices produced by Prim's algorithm has $n-1$ edges. In fact, any tree with n vertices has $n-1$ edges; this is Result 2.

Result 2   Any tree with n vertices has precisely $n-1$ edges.

Justification

Let S be any tree with n vertices. Then S is a connected graph, so, by Result 1, S must have a spanning subtree, T, with $n-1$ edges.

If $S = T$, then there is nothing to prove. So suppose that S has at least one edge other than those in T, and suppose this edge connects vertex v to vertex w (see Fig. 3.19). But T is connected, so w is connected to v by a path of edges in T. Then, in S, there is a cycle.

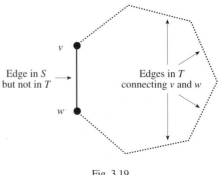

Edge in S but not in T Edges in T connecting v and w

But S is a tree and so contains no cycles. Thus the supposition that S has at least one edge other than those in T leads to a contradiction. Thus the only possibility is $S = T$.

Fig. 3.19

Result 1 shows that, for any connected graph with n vertices, Prim's algorithm will produce a spanning tree. It only remains to show that it always finds a spanning tree of minimum weight.

In the justification of Result 3 you may find it helpful to refer to the example in Fig. 3.20. However, the proof that Prim's algorithm gives a tree of minimum weight is general, and does not rely on the diagrams.

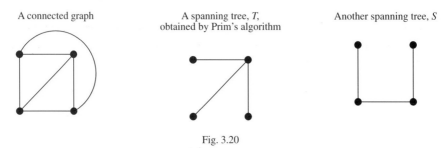

Fig. 3.20

For the example in Fig. 3.20, T_1, T_2, T_3 and T_4 are as shown in Fig. 3.21.

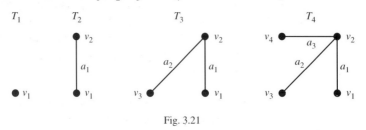

Fig. 3.21

Result 3   Let S be any spanning tree for a connected graph and let T be a spanning tree produced by Prim's algorithm. Then $\text{weight}(T) \leqslant \text{weight}(S)$.

Justification

The spanning tree S contains T_1. If S contains T_n, which is the same as T, then there is nothing to prove, so suppose that S contains T_k but not T_{k+1}. Thus a_k is not an edge of S.

Using the example, Fig. 3.22 shows the case when $k = 2$. Here S contains T_2 but not T_3.

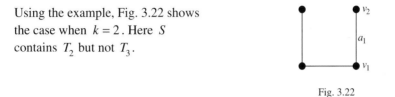

Fig. 3.22

Add edge a_k to S. As S was a tree there is now a cycle containing the edge a_k. This edge a_k joins a vertex of T_k to a vertex outside T_k so there is at least one other edge of the cycle, f say, which joins a vertex of T_k to a vertex outside T_k. Remove edge f to form a new graph, S'.

Fig. 3.23 shows how this works with the example.

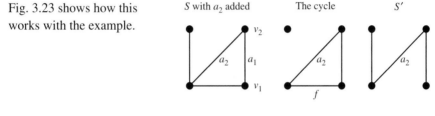

Fig. 3.23

Edge f was part of a cycle so removing f does not disconnect the graph. S' is therefore a new spanning tree which contains T_{k+1}.

Since a_k was chosen to be the kth edge by Prim's algorithm, its weight is less than or equal to the weight of any other edge which joins a vertex of T_k to a vertex outside T_k. In particular,

$$\text{weight}(a_k) \leqslant \text{weight}(f),$$

and

$$\text{weight}(S') = \text{weight}(S) + \text{weight}(a_k) - \text{weight}(f) \leqslant \text{weight}(S).$$

By repeating this process as necessary, you can successively replace edges of S by edges of T, without increasing the weight. Eventually all $n-1$ edges of S will have been replaced by the $n-1$ edges of T and so the weight of T must be less than or equal to the weight of S. As this is true whatever spanning tree is used for starting the process, T is a minimum spanning tree.

This completes the justification that Prim's algorithm always produces a minimum spanning tree. Note that the minimum spanning tree need not be unique. There could be more than one, but they would all have the same weight.

Example 3.6.1
Look at Fig. 3.24. For the connected graph at the left, use the method of Result 3 to replace the edges of the spanning tree S by those of spanning tree T, produced by Prim's algorithm.

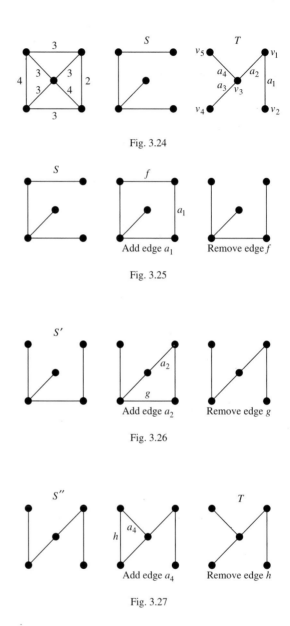

Fig. 3.24

The first edge in T which is not in S is a_1. Add a_1 to S. Then remove edge f from the cycle formed. This is shown in Fig. 3.25. Call the new spanning tree S'.

Fig. 3.25

This increases the weight by 2, and then reduces it by 3.

The next edge in T which is not in the new spanning tree S' is a_2. Add a_2, and then remove edge g from the cycle formed. This is shown in Fig. 3.26. Call the new spanning tree S''.

Fig. 3.26

This increases the weight by 3, and reduces it by 3.

The next edge in T which is not in the new spanning tree S'' is a_4. (Note that a_3 is already in the new spanning tree.) Add a_4, and then remove edge h from the cycle formed. This is shown in Fig. 3.27.

Fig. 3.27

This increases the weight by 3, and reduces it by 4. The net result of the process is to obtain T, with a weight of 2 less than S.

Try removing one of the other possible edges in place of f in the first stage, and see what happens subsequently.

Miscellaneous exercise 3

1 The table shows the distances in miles between six US cities.

	C	Da	De	LA	NY	W
Chicago	–	800	900	1800	700	650
Dallas	800	–	650	1300	1350	1200
Denver	900	650	–	850	1650	1500
Los Angeles	1800	1300	850	–	2500	2350
New York	700	1350	1650	2500	–	200
Washington DC	650	1200	1500	2350	200	–

Use Prim's algorithm to find the minimum connector. Draw the minimum spanning tree and find its total length.

2 The gardens of a stately home are to be opened to the public. The distances, in metres, between various features are as shown in the table.

	A	B	C	D	E	F	G
A	–	250	200	–	500	300	–
B	250	–	400	200	–	70	–
C	200	400	–	300	400	–	300
D	–	200	300	–	–	–	350
E	500	–	400	–	–	–	500
F	300	70	–	–	–	–	–
G	–	–	300	350	500	–	–

(a) Use Prim's algorithm to determine the shortest possible length of pathway to enable visitors to walk between all of the features.

(b) The owners decide to build an ornamental lake between features A and C, so that there is no route between them. What effect does this have on the shortest possible length of pathway?

3 Draw the network which is tabulated in Question 2. Hence apply Kruskal's algorithm, showing your working clearly.

4 A connected graph G has five vertices. The lengths of the edges are 7, 7, 7, 9, 11, 12, 13, 15 and 16 units, respectively.

(a) A graph is said to be *fully connected* if every vertex is joined at least once to every other vertex. Explain why this graph G cannot be fully connected.

(b) A connected graph G is to be drawn with 5 vertices with lengths of edges as given above.

    (i) Calculate the least possible length of a minimum spanning tree of graph G.

    (ii) Explain why your answer to part (b)(i) might not apply to graph G.

    (iii) Sketch an example of graph G which has a minimum spanning tree of length 34 units. (AQA)

5 Adapt Kruskal's algorithm so as to produce an algorithm which will find the spanning tree of *greatest* weight. Apply your algorithm to the network of distances, in kilometres, between towns shown in the diagram.

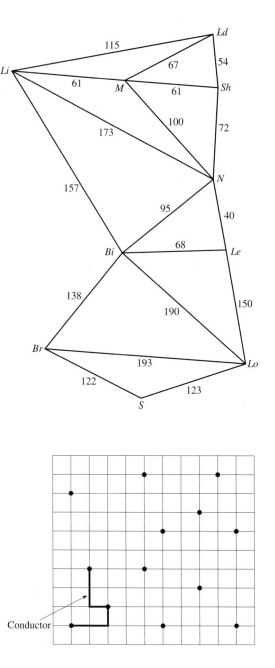

6 The diagram shows a set of holes drilled through a printed circuit board which has a 1 cm grid drawn on it. These need to be joined together using the shortest possible length of conductor. The conductor can only be laid parallel to the sides of the printed circuit board.

(a) Find the least possible length of conductor, given that two lengths of conductor may only meet at the drilled holes; that is, no new vertices can be created. (Part of the conductor is shown drawn in.)

(b) By how much can the length of conductor be reduced if new vertices may be created?

7 A company has offices in six towns. The costs, in £, of travelling between these towns are shown in the table below.

	A	B	C	D	E	F
A	–	15	26	13	14	25
B	15	–	16	16	25	13
C	26	16	–	38	16	15
D	13	16	38	–	15	19
E	14	25	16	15	–	14
F	25	13	15	19	14	–

(a) Use Prim's algorithm, starting by deleting row A, to find the cheapest way of visiting the six towns. You should show all your working and indicate the order in which the towns were included.

The travel times, in minutes, between the six towns are given in the table below.

	A	B	C	D	E	F
A	–	20	30	20	10	30
B	20	–	20	30	20	10
C	30	20	–	30	30	30
D	20	30	30	–	10	30
E	10	20	30	10	–	10
F	30	10	30	30	10	–

(b) The company wants it to be possible to travel from any town to any other town in under an hour. Show that this is not possible if they just use the edges from the solution to part (a).

(c) Construct the minimum connector tree for the travel times. Work out how much it would cost to travel from A to C, using just these edges, and how long it would take.

(OCR)

8 (a) Write down the matrix that represents the network shown in the figure.

(b) Apply Prim's algorithm to this matrix, starting by crossing out row A, to find the edges that make up a minimum connector for this network. Show all your working clearly, and indicate the order in which you build your minimum connector.

(c) Write down the length of your minimum connector.

(OCR)

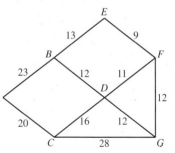

9 The following matrix shows the distances, in miles, between six towns.

	A	B	C	D	E	F
A	–	12	20	14	15	25
B	12	–	23	7	13	8
C	20	23	–	16	16	12
D	14	7	16	–	20	9
E	15	13	16	20	–	15
F	25	8	12	9	15	–

(a) Using Kruskal's algorithm and showing your working at each stage, find the minimum spanning tree for these six towns.

(b) State the length of your minimum spanning tree.   (AQA)

10 (a) For a connected graph with n vertices, state the number of edges in a minimum spanning tree.

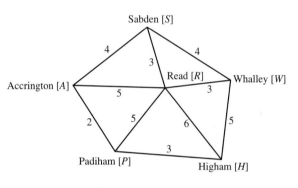

(b) A cable company has laid cables to Accrington and is now considering extending the network to neighbouring villages. The distances, in miles,

between the villages are shown.

(i) Using Prim's algorithm, showing a sketch at each stage, obtain the minimum spanning tree for the cable company.

(ii) State the length of your minimum spanning tree.   (AQA)

11 In the network shown, the weights on the edges represent lengths.

(a) Use an efficient algorithm (not complete enumeration) to find a minimum connector for the network. Show your working and give your minimum connector and its length.

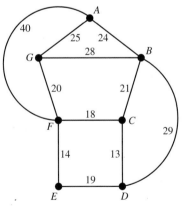

(b) Apply the following algorithm to the network. State what happens at each step, give the result, and state what the algorithm achieves.

  1. Select a longest edge.

  2. Remove the edge which has just been selected if doing so leaves the network connected.

  3. Stop if all remaining edges have been selected.

  4. Select a longest edge which has not yet been selected, and go to step 2.   (AQA)

4 Finding the shortest path

This chapter is about finding the path between two vertices which has the least weight. When you have completed it you should

- be able to apply the method known as Dijkstra's algorithm
- be aware of the circumstances under which Dijkstra's algorithm can be applied.

4.1 'Shortest'

It is now relatively inexpensive to buy a route planner for a private car. With this you can find the route to your destination which has the shortest distance, or which takes the least time based upon the latest traffic information and expected speeds on different roads. The same algorithm will solve both of these problems; in one case you must consider the network of distances, and in the other case you must consider the network of times. This type of problem is generally known as a 'shortest path' problem but it is better thought of as a problem of finding the path of minimum weight. The weights of edges may be distances or times, as above, or they could be something entirely different, such as depreciation costs or petrol charges.

The map in Fig. 4.1 shows the main routes between six towns. Single lines are A-roads, and double lines are motorways.

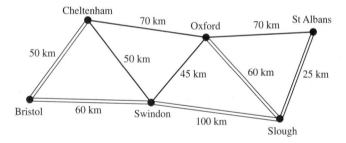

Fig. 4.1

Try to solve the following problems by inspection before looking at the solutions (page 125).

1 What is the shortest path from St Albans to Bristol?

2 Suppose the average speed on the A-roads to be 80 km h^{-1} and on the motorways to be 110 km h^{-1}. What is the quickest route from St Albans to Cheltenham?

3 Suppose further that there is a quarter of an hour delay on the M25 from St Albans to Slough. What now is the quickest route from St Albans to Bristol?

As shortest path questions become more complicated it soon becomes necessary to develop a systematic approach to solving them. One of the most commonly used methods for the shortest path problem is an algorithm invented by Edsger Dijkstra.

4.2 Dijkstra's algorithm

This algorithm is based upon the idea of labelling each vertex with the length of the shortest path from the start vertex found so far. This temporary label is replaced whenever a shorter path is found. When you can be certain that there is no shorter route you 'box' the label to show that it is now a **permanent label**.

Dijkstra's algorithm

Step 1 Label the start vertex with zero and box this label.

Step 2 Consider the vertex with the most recently boxed label. Suppose this vertex to be X and let D be its permanent label. Then, in turn, consider each vertex directly joined to X but not yet permanently boxed. For each such vertex, Y say, temporarily label it with the lesser of $D +$ (the weight of edge XY) and its existing label (if any).

Step 3 Choose the least of all temporary labels on the network. Make this label permanent by boxing it.

Step 4 Repeat Steps 2 and 3 until the destination vertex has a permanent label.

Step 5 Go backwards through the network, retracing the path of shortest length from the destination vertex to the start vertex.

Example 4.2.1

Find the shortest path from A to G in Fig. 4.2.

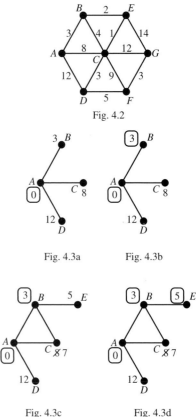

Fig. 4.3a shows the situation after Step 1, in which A was labelled 0 and boxed, and the first pass through Step 2, where B, C and D have temporary labels.

In Step 3, the least of the temporary labels is at B, so this is made permanent by boxing it, as shown in Fig. 4.3b.

Fig. 4.3c shows the situation after the next pass through Step 2, where the temporary label 5 on E comes from adding the most recently boxed label, 3 at B, and the length 2 from B to E. Similarly, the temporary label at C comes from adding the permanent label 3 at B and the length 4 from B to C to make a total of 7. As 7 is less than the existing temporary label 8 at C, the 8 is crossed out and replaced with 7.

Fig. 4.3d shows the label at E boxed, as it is the least of the temporary labels. This provides the starting point for the next pass through Step 2.

Continuing in this way, you eventually get to the point at which all the labels are permanently boxed. This is shown in Fig. 4.4.

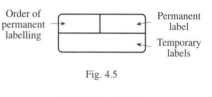

Fig. 4.4

You are now ready for Step 5.

Retracing the path backwards through the network, you can see that

17_G was produced by $14_F + 3$.

14_F was produced by $9_D + 5$, and so on.

The shortest path is $ABECDFG$, which has length 17.

Note that a bonus of Dijkstra's algorithm is that once the algorithm has been carried out you know the shortest paths to all permanently labelled vertices.

If you are required to show the order of permanent labelling, it can be useful to put your working at each vertex in a box, as shown in Fig. 4.5.

Fig. 4.5

Thus, the box in Fig. 4.6 shows that the relevant vertex received an initial temporary label of 8, then one of 7, and finally one of 5. This became its permanent label, and it was the 6th vertex to be permanently labelled.

Fig. 4.6

Example 4.2.2

The network shown in Fig. 4.7 represents part of a road system in a city. Some of the roads are one-way, and the weights on the edges represent estimated travel times, in minutes. What is the quickest route from A to K?

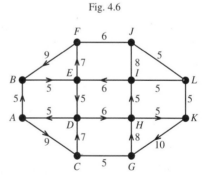

Fig. 4.7

Fig. 4.8 shows the result of applying Dijkstra's algorithm.

Retracing the steps, you find that the quickest route is $ABEDHK$, taking a total time of 26 minutes.

Notice that you need not draw a new diagram for each pass through Dijkstra's algorithm.

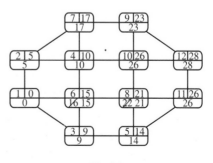

Fig. 4.8

Exercise 4

1 Use Dijkstra's algorithm to find the shortest path from A to G for the network shown below. Show how you arrive at your result.

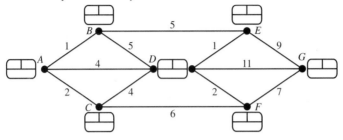

2 Use Dijkstra's algorithm to find the shortest path from A to J for the network below.

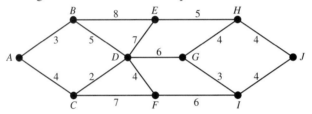

3 The table shows the cost in £ of direct journeys between six towns. Find the minimum cost of travelling from A to F.

	A	B	C	D	E	F
A	–	11	12	–	–	–
B	11	–	–	15	18	–
C	12	–	–	8	21	–
D	–	15	8	–	–	20
E	–	18	21	–	–	15
F	–	–	–	20	15	–

4 Each move of a counter is one square horizontally or vertically on the board shown here. The counter cannot move across the thick lines.

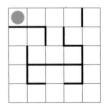

Apply Dijkstra's algorithm to find the smallest number of moves from the square marked with a counter to each other square.

5 Moore's algorithm for a connected graph with two specified vertices, m and n, is as follows.

Step 1 Let $i = 0$.

Step 2 Label m with 0.

Step 3 Find all unlabelled vertices that are adjacent to a vertex labelled i, and label them $i + 1$.

Step 4 Replace i by $i + 1$.

Step 5 Repeat Steps 3 and 4 until vertex n is labelled.

(a) Apply Moore's algorithm to the graph in the figure.

(b) What is Moore's algorithm designed to accomplish?

(c) What is the connection between Moore's algorithm and Dijkstra's algorithm?

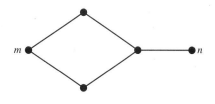

4.3   A drawback of Dijkstra's algorithm

One drawback of Dijkstra's algorithm is that it cannot be used if any weights are negative. (The cost of a route might be negative if, for example, a firm could achieve a profit by making a delivery along that route.)

Example 4.3.1

(a) What is the shortest route from A to C in the network of Fig. 4.9?

(b) What is the result of applying Dijkstra's algorithm?

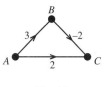

Fig. 4.9

(a) You can see by inspection that the shortest route is ABC, which has weight 1.

(b) Fig. 4.10 shows the effect of applying Dijkstra's algorithm. The problem is that vertex C is permanently labelled before the route ABC is considered.

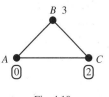

Fig. 4.10

Similarly, Dijkstra's algorithm cannot be used for longest path problems.

Miscellaneous exercise 4

1 (a) Use Dijkstra's algorithm to
        find the shortest path from A
        to F. Show all necessary
        working.

   (b) A directed edge from C to
        D is now added, with weight
        -4. What is the shortest path
        from A to F now? Explain
        why Dijkstra's algorithm can-
        not be used to find this path.

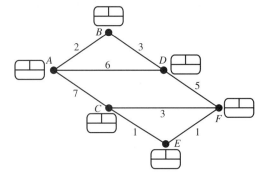

2 The numbers on the diagram represent the times in
   minutes of the journeys between railway stations.

   (a) What is the quickest route from A to D?

   (b) How could you adjust the numbers to model
        the fact that there is a delay of 20 minutes
        on all journeys passing through station O?

        What is now the quickest route from A to D?

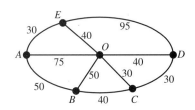

3 It is required to find the
   shortest paths from each of
   A, B and C to N.

   (a) How can these paths be
        determined by applying
        Dijkstra's algorithm just
        once?

   (b) Obtain the three shortest
        paths. Which of A, B
        and C is nearest to N?

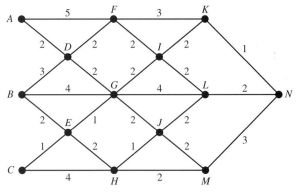

4 Fares (in £) for direct flights between five cities are shown in the table.

	A	B	C	D	E
A	–	90	70	35	30
B	90	–	40	150	55
C	70	40	–	20	50
D	35	150	20	–	100
E	30	55	50	100	–

   (a) Draw a network and use Dijkstra's algorithm to find the cheapest routes from A to
        each other city.

   (b) Suppose each change of flight is estimated to cost an extra £10 of sundry expenses.
        Find the cheapest routes now.

5 The numbers on the edges of this network represent the maximum weight (in tons) of a vehicle allowed on the road that the edge represents.

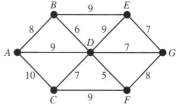

(a) What is the heaviest vehicle that can travel from A to G?

(b) How can Dijkstra's algorithm be modified to solve problems of this type?

6 Apply Dijkstra's algorithm to find the shortest path from A to I.

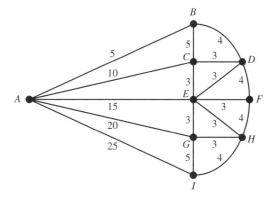

7 Use Dijkstra's algorithm to find the length of the shortest path from A to B.

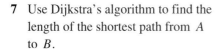

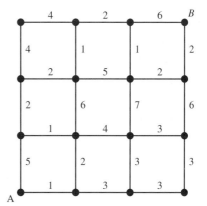

8 The network shows the times, in minutes, of train journeys between seven stations.

(a) Given that there is no time delay in passing through a station, use Dijkstra's algorithm to find the shortest time to travel from A to G.

(b) Find the shortest time to travel from A to G, if, in reality, each time the train passes through a station excluding A and G, an extra 10 minutes is added to the journey time.

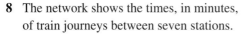

(AQA)

9 The owner of a stately home is concerned that wheelchair access to his property is limited. Currently it is impossible to visit the upper floor, the servants' quarters, the chapel, the lake and the tower in a wheelchair; all other parts of the house and its grounds are accessible.

The costs (in £1000s) of installing ramps or lifts to connect the various parts of the property are shown in the table below. X means that a direct connection is not possible.

	House and grounds	Upper floor	Servants' quarters	Chapel	Lake	Tower
House and grounds	–	3	5	7	7	6
Upper floor	3	–	1	X	X	2
Servants' quarters	5	1	–	2	4	X
Chapel	7	X	2	–	6	3
Lake	7	X	4	6	–	1
Tower	6	2	X	3	1	–

(a) Draw a network to represent this information.

(b) Use Dijkstra's algorithm to find the cheapest way of connecting each of the five areas to the house and grounds. Show all your working clearly, and indicate the order in which you assign permanent labels to vertices.

(c) Use the solution to part (b) to list which connections should be made for wheelchair users to be able to reach all parts of the property, at minimum cost to the owner. Explain how you knew which edges to include, and find the cost of making these connections.

(d) Explain what is special about the edges that make up the solution, and name an algorithm that could have been used to find the solution in a more direct way.   (OCR)

10 Little Red Riding Hood wants to travel through the woods from her house, at point A, to Grandma's house, at point G. The network shows the possible paths that she may use, and the time (in minutes) to travel each path.

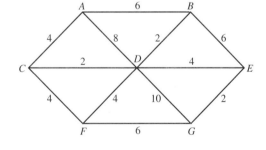

(a) Use Dijkstra's algorithm to find the quickest route from A to G. Show all your working clearly, and indicate the order in which you assign permanent labels to vertices.

(b) The big bad wolf also wants to travel from A to G. He knows which route Little Red Riding Hood has chosen, and he must avoid using any of the edges on her route.

Find the quickest route from A to G for the big bad wolf.

(c) The big bad wolf travels twice as quickly as Little Red Riding Hood. Assuming that Little Red Riding Hood and the big bad wolf leave A at the same time, and that they use the routes found above, work out how long the big bad wolf will have to wait at Grandma's house before Little Red Riding Hood arrives.   (OCR)

11 The table shows the distances (in metres) of the shortest direct route between each of seven classrooms, A, B, C, D, E, F and G.

	A	B	C	D	E	F	G
A	0	200	50	35	65	80	250
B	200	0	150	200	120	100	25
C	50	150	0	10	5	25	150
D	35	200	10	0	20	40	200
E	65	120	5	20	0	10	100
F	80	100	25	40	10	0	100
G	250	25	150	200	100	100	0

(a) Use Dijkstra's algorithm to find the shortest distance from classroom A to classroom B. Show all your working clearly, and indicate the order in which you assign permanent labels to the vertices.

The teacher in classroom A asks a pupil to take a message to each of the other classrooms, and then come back to classroom A.

(b) Use your answer to part (a) to find an upper bound for the shortest route that the pupil can take. (OCR)

12 The figure shows a network of roads connecting seven farms. The values shown represent the times, in minutes, to travel along the roads.

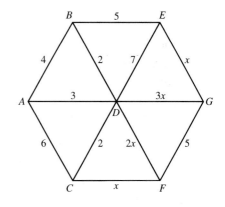

(a) Given that $x > 1$, use Dijkstra's algorithm to show that the two possible expressions, in terms of x, for the minimum time to travel from A to F are

$3 + 2x$ and $5 + x$.

(b) (i) Find the three possible expressions, in terms of x, for the minimum time to travel from A to G.

(ii) Given that the route ADG is found to be the quickest, find the range of possible values of x. (AQA, adapted)

5 Matching

This chapter is about matching the elements of one set with elements of another. When you have completed it you should

- be aware of the relevance of bipartite graphs
- be able to express matching problems in assignment matrix form
- be able to apply the Matching Augmentation algorithm.

5.1 Introduction

In Chapter 2 you met very briefly the idea of a bipartite graph.

> A **bipartite graph** is a graph with two sets of vertices such that edges only connect vertices from one set to the other and do not connect vertices within a set.

It is convenient to always consider the two sets of vertices of a bipartite graph to be the **left-vertices** and the **right-vertices**. For example, $K_{3,3}$ would be drawn as shown in Fig. 5.1.

One of the main applications of bipartite graphs is to **assignment problems** in which the task is to pair up the maximum possible number of left-vertices and right-vertices.

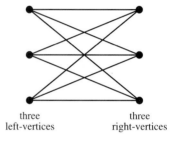

three
left-vertices

three
right-vertices

Fig. 5.1

You have already met an assignment problem in Exercise 2A Question 8.

Example 5.1.1

Four Members of Parliament, Ann, Brian, Clare and David, are being considered for four cabinet posts. Ann could be Foreign Secretary or Home Secretary, Brian could be Home Secretary or the Chancellor of the Exchequer, Clare could be Foreign Secretary or the Minister for Education and David could be the Chancellor or the Home Secretary.

(a) Draw a bipartite graph to represent this situation.

(b) How many options does the Prime Minister have?

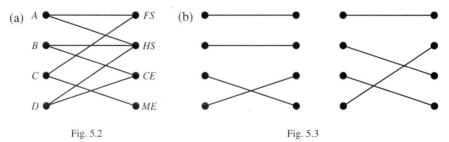

Fig. 5.2   Fig. 5.3

Fig. 5.2 shows the graph, and Fig. 5.3 shows the two options.

Two definitions which are used in assignment problems are:

> For any bipartite graph, a **matching** is a set of
> edges which have no vertices in common.
>
> A **maximum matching** is any matching which
> contains the largest possible number of edges.

The maximum matching of Example 5.1.1 covered all of the vertices and is called a
complete matching. A complete matching is not always possible.

Example 5.1.2

Four couples are booked into a small hotel. The Smiths have requested a double room
and the Joneses have asked for a double room on the ground floor. The Browns require a
twin-bedded room and the Greens will be happy with any room on the ground floor. The
hotel manager has just four rooms to assign, three double and one twin-bedded. The
twin-bedded room and one of the doubles is on the ground floor. Can the manager
satisfy the requirements of all the couples?

The relevant bipartite graph is shown in Fig. 5.4.

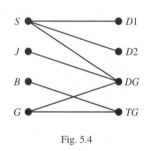

The requirements of the Joneses, Browns and
Greens cannot all be satisfied, because the
Smiths are the only couple who are content with
the double rooms which are not on the ground
floor, and they cannot use both of them. The
maximum matching has three pairings. One
example is $\{S, D1\}, \{J, DG\}, \{B, TG\}$.

Fig. 5.4

As well as representing the information in assignment problems by bipartite graphs, you
can also use **adjacency matrices**.

The left-vertices are put down one side, and the
right-vertices along the top. An entry of 1
means that the corresponding vertices are
linked by an edge.

$$\begin{array}{c} \quad D1\ D2\ DG\ TG \\ \begin{array}{c}S\\J\\B\\G\end{array}\left(\begin{array}{cccc}1&1&1&0\\0&0&1&0\\0&0&0&1\\0&0&1&1\end{array}\right)\end{array}$$

Fig. 5.5

For example, the matrix in Fig. 5.5 contains the
same information as the graph of Fig. 5.4.

For a problem formulated as an adjacency
matrix, the task is to find the maximum number
of 1s such that no two of these 1s are in the
same row or in the same column. In Fig. 5.6 the
solution is shown by the 1s in bold-faced type.
If you were solving this problem you would
probably wish to ring the 1s in the solution.

$$\left(\begin{array}{cccc}\mathbf{1}&1&1&0\\0&0&\mathbf{1}&0\\0&0&0&\mathbf{1}\\0&0&1&1\end{array}\right)$$

Fig. 5.6

5.2 The Matching Augmentation algorithm

In the previous section you solved simple matching problems by inspection. As the numbers of vertices and edges increase, inspection becomes a hit or miss affair and the chance of overlooking a maximum matching grows.

Fortunately, there is a simple algorithm which can be used to improve upon (or augment) an initial matching or to show that you have already obtained a maximum matching. Consider the following example. Although this has only 10 vertices, it is nevertheless difficult to spot a maximum matching. This example will be used to illustrate the Matching Augmentation algorithm.

Example 5.2.1

A builder employs five workers: Alan, who does labouring, plastering and joinery; Betty, who does labouring and wiring; Colin, who does bricklaying and wiring; Di, who does plastering and bricklaying; and Ed, who does plastering, joinery and bricklaying. Can all five workers be assigned to tasks so that all five tasks are covered?

First, draw a bipartite graph for this problem. In Fig. 5.7, the heavy lines represent a first try at a matching, which assigns just four workers to tasks.

The Matching Augmentation algorithm will show how to improve this matching, if it is possible.

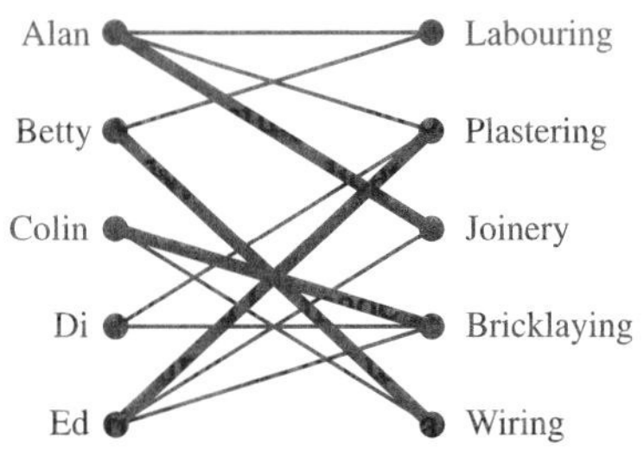

Fig. 5.7

The Matching Augmentation algorithm

Step 1 Consider all edges of the matching to be directed from right to left. Consider all other edges to be directed from left to right.

Step 2 Create a new vertex, X say, joined with directed edges to all left-vertices which do not belong to the matching.

Step 3 Give each edge a weighting of 1.

Step 4 Apply Dijkstra's algorithm from X until one of the following happens

- a right-vertex which does not belong to the matching is reached

- no further labelling is possible. In this case, the initial matching cannot be improved and the algorithm stops.

Step 5 Retrace any path from an unmatched left-vertex to the unmatched right-vertex.

Step 6 Remove from the original matching any edges in the path of Step 5. Add to the matching the other steps in the path. This increases, by 1, the number of edges in the matching.

The result of applying the first four
steps of the Matching
Augmentation algorithm to
Example 5.2.1 is shown in Fig. 5.8.

You can see that all the paths have
been given directions, as required
in Step 1.

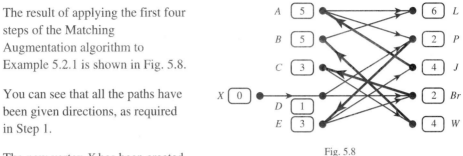

Fig. 5.8

The new vertex X has been created
and joined to D, a left-vertex which does not belong to the initial matching.

Dijkstra's algorithm was then applied from X, and the right-vertex L, which doesn't
belong to the initial matching, is reached. At this stage Step 4 has been completed.

*Note that the algorithm requires only the simplified version of Dijkstra's algorithm,
called Moore's algorithm, given in Exercise 4A Question 5.*

To carry out Step 5, you need to trace a path from D to L: there are two
possibilities, D-P-E-J-A-L and D-Br-C-W-B-L, and you could choose either one.

Looking at the first of these, as you trace the path, you cover P-E and J-A, both of
which were in the initial matching. Remove them from the initial matching, and
add the other edges from the path, D-P, E-J and A-L, to the initial matching. This
increases by 1 the number of edges in the matching. In this case, the matching is
now maximal. It is

$$A\text{-}L, \quad B\text{-}W, \quad C\text{-}Br, \quad D\text{-}P, \quad E\text{-}J.$$

If you had chosen the other path, D-Br-C-W-B-L, you would cover Br-C and W-B from
the initial matching. If you removed them, and replaced them by D-Br, C-W and B-L,
the new matching would have become

$$A\text{-}J, \quad B\text{-}L, \quad C\text{-}W, \quad D\text{-}Br, \quad E\text{-}P,$$

an alternative maximal matching.

The next example illustrates how the Matching Augmentation algorithm recognises that
a maximum matching has already been reached.

Example 5.2.2
A school timetabling team is trying to timetable four teachers, Andy, Barbara, Chris and
Dave to four classes, denoted by R, S, T and U.

Andy can teach R or S Barbara can teach R, S, T or U
Chris can teach R or S Dave can teach S.

Draw a bipartite graph and apply the Matching Augmentation algorithm to find a
maximum matching.

An initial attempt at a matching is illustrated by the heavy lines in Fig. 5.9.

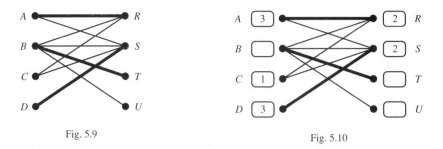

Fig. 5.9   Fig. 5.10

The result of applying the Matching Augmentation algorithm is then shown in Fig. 5.10. The label X that was initially created and then joined to C is not shown.

No further labelling is possible, so the initial matching is maximum. Notice that although it is maximal it is not complete.

Exercise 5

1   Apply the Matching Augmentation algorithm to the following bipartite graphs where the heavy lines represent matchings. In each case state what you can conclude.

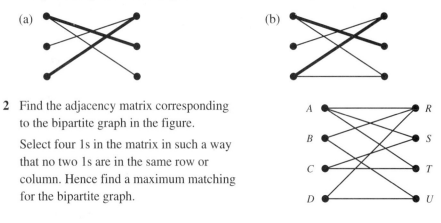

(a)   (b)

2   Find the adjacency matrix corresponding to the bipartite graph in the figure.

Select four 1s in the matrix in such a way that no two 1s are in the same row or column. Hence find a maximum matching for the bipartite graph.

3   The adjacency matrix shown below represents an incomplete matching.

$$
\begin{array}{c}
\quad\;\; E\;\; F\;\; G\;\; H \\
\begin{array}{c}A\\B\\C\\D\end{array}
\left(\begin{array}{cccc}
1 & 0 & 1 & 0 \\
0 & 1 & 1 & 0 \\
1 & 0 & 1 & 1 \\
1 & 1 & 1 & 0
\end{array}\right)
\end{array}
$$

(a)   Draw a bipartite graph to represent the possible pairings and to show the incomplete matching.

(b)   Use the Matching Augmentation algorithm to obtain a complete matching. Explain your method carefully.

4 A large department store employs five students, Anita, Bruce, Chloe, Darminder and Errol, for the Christmas period.

The Hardware manager would be happy to use Anita, Chloe or Darminder.
The Book-shop manager would be happy to use Bruce or Errol.
The Sports manager would be happy to use Anita or Darminder.
The Electrical manager would be happy to use Darminder or Errol.
The Foodhall manager would be happy to use Anita or Chloe.

(a) Draw a bipartite graph, G, to show which students are suitable for each department.

The managing director initially decides to place Anita in the Foodhall, Chloe in Hardware, Darminder in Electrical and Errol in the Book-shop. However, he is then unable to place Bruce appropriately.

(b) Show the incomplete matching, M, that describes the managing director's attempted allocation.

(c) Use the Matching Augmentation algorithm to construct an alternating path for M in G, and hence find a maximum matching.

5 A dance team consists of four men, Ahmed, Barry, Chris and Derek, paired with four women, Ann, Bala, Celine and Di. Ann is only prepared to dance with Ahmed, Bala will dance with Barry or Derek, Celine will dance with Chris, and Di will dance with any of the men. In their first competition, Di dances with Derek.

(a) Draw a bipartite graph to represent the only possible matching with Di and Derek paired. Unfortunately, Di and Derek fall out and a different pairing has to be arranged for the second competition.

(b) Draw a bipartite graph to show the possible pairings and the incomplete matching, M, from the first competition.

(c) Apply the Matching Augmentation algorithm to obtain a complete matching for the second competition.

5.3* Maximum matching – minimum cover

There is an important connection between the matching problem and the problem of finding sets of vertices which cover every edge, that is, sets of vertices which contain at least one end-vertex of each edge of the bipartite graph. These are called **cover sets** of the graph.

Consider, for example, the graph drawn for Example 5.2.2, redrawn as Fig. 5.11.

Since A-R, B-T and D-S is a matching, a cover set must contain at least one of A or R, at least one of B or T and at least one of D or S.

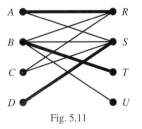
Fig. 5.11

In general it is clear that:

> The number of edges in any matching $\leqslant$ the number of vertices in any cover set.

The smallest possible number of vertices in a cover set cannot, therefore, be less than the number of edges in a maximum matching. In Example 5.2.2, this minimum is actually achieved for the cover set $\{B, R, S\}$. The interesting aspect of the connection between the matching problem and the cover set problem is that this result is always true. That is:

The number of edges in   the minimum number of
a maximum matching   =   vertices in a cover set.

This result can be proved by considering the effect of applying the Matching Augmentation algorithm to bipartite graphs for which the maximum matching has already been achieved.

Consider, for example, the following examples:

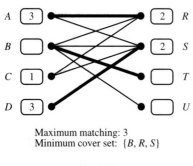

Maximum matching: 3
Minimum cover set: $\{B, R, S\}$

Fig. 5.12

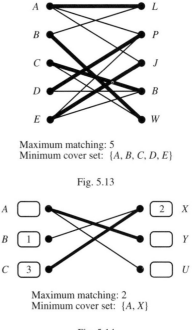

Maximum matching: 5
Minimum cover set: $\{A, B, C, D, E\}$

Fig. 5.13

The key to proving the maximum matching – minimum cover result is to note how the examples of cover sets in Fig. 5.12 to Fig. 5.14 are formed. In each case, they consist of the unlabelled left-vertices and labelled right-vertices.

Maximum matching: 2
Minimum cover set: $\{A, X\}$

Fig. 5.14

To prove the maximum matching – minimum cover result it is therefore necessary to prove:

- the unlabelled left-vertices and labelled right-vertices form a cover set;
- the number of these vertices equals the number of edges in a maximum matching.

These two facts follow from the following features of maximum matchings to which the Matching Augmentation algorithm has been applied. In each case, you should try to explain the reason for these features (see Miscellaneous exercise 5 Question 6).

- Each edge of the bipartite graph either has an unlabelled left-vertex or a labelled right-vertex.
- All unlabelled left-vertices are in the matching.

- All labelled right-vertices are in the matching.
- Each edge of the matching joins vertices which are either both labelled or both unlabelled.

Then:

Number of edges of maximum matching

= number of right-vertices of matching

= number of unlabelled right-vertices of matching +
  number of labelled right-vertices of matching

= number of unlabelled left - vertices of matching +
  number of labelled right-vertices of matching

= number of unlabelled left-vertices + number of labelled right-vertices

= number of vertices in a cover set.

The maximum matching – minimum cover result can be useful for seeing quickly that a maximum matching has been found and that there is no need to apply the Matching Augmentation algorithm.

Example 5.3.1

For the bipartite graph shown in Fig. 5.15, find
(a) a cover set containing four vertices,
(b) a matching containing four edges.
What can you conclude from your answers to
(a) and (b)?

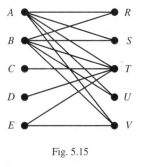

Fig. 5.15

 (a) $A, B, T, V.$

 (b) $\{A, R\}. \{B, S\}, \{C, T\}, \{E, V\}.$

Hence the solution to part (b) is actually a maximum matching.

Miscellaneous exercise 5

1 A university mathematics lecturer is organising her six students into pairs to work on a mathematical modelling exercise. She would like to arrange it so that no students who have previously worked together are doing so on this exercise. So far

  a has worked with b, d and e, b has worked with a, d and f,
  c has worked with d, e and f, d has worked with a, b and c,
  e has worked with a, c and f,   and f has worked with b, c and e.

 (a) Draw a graph, G, to represent this information.

 (b) Draw a graph on six vertices which consists of all those edges which are in K_6 but not in G. Say how this will help the lecturer.   (AQA, adapted)

2 In a mixed badminton tournament, four men, Arnold, Barry, Charles and Derek, must be paired with four women, Jane, Kate, Lorna and Marie.

- Arnold may be paired with Jane, Kate or Lorna, but not Marie.
- Barry may be paired with Kate only.
- Charles may be paired with Kate or Marie, but not Jane or Lorna.
- Derek may be paired with Jane or Marie, but not Kate or Lorna.

(a) Draw a bipartite graph, G, showing which men may be paired with which women.

Jane decides to pair with Arnold, Kate decides to pair with Barry and Marie decides to pair with Derek. This leaves Lorna and Charles, who will not agree to be paired.

(b) On your graph, G, show the incomplete matching, M, described above.

(c) Use a matching algorithm to construct an alternating path for M in G, explaining your method carefully, and hence obtain a complete matching between the men and the women.   (OCR)

3 Jim is spending a week on holiday at Spaceworld. The table lists the planets that he wants to visit, and the days that these planets are open for visitors. Jim wants to visit one planet each day.

Mercury	Saturday and Monday
Venus	Saturday, Sunday and Monday
Earth	Monday, Tuesday and Wednesday
Mars	Monday and Friday
Jupiter	Wednesday and Thursday
Saturn	Tuesday
Uranus	Sunday and Friday

Jim arrived at Spaceworld on Saturday, and immediately went to visit Mercury. On Sunday he visited Venus and on Monday he visited Earth.

Jim then realised that he would not be able to visit all seven planets on his list in the week. He decided that he would leave out visiting Uranus, and that he would have a free day on Thursday.

(a) Draw a bipartite graph showing which planets are open on which days, and use it to show the incomplete matching that Jim chose.

(b) Use a matching algorithm to construct an alternating path, and hence find a maximal matching between the planets and the days.   (AQA)

4   Granny has bought Christmas presents for her five grandchildren.

>   The teddy bear is suitable for Cathy, Daniel or Elvis;
>   the book is suitable for Annie or Ben;
>   the football is suitable for Daniel or Elvis;
>   the money box is suitable for Annie or Daniel;
>   the drum is suitable for Cathy or Elvis.

Draw a bipartite graph, G, to show which present is suitable for which grandchild.

Granny decides to give Annie the book, Cathy the teddy bear, Daniel the money box and Elvis the drum. This leaves Ben without a present, since the football is not suitable for him.

(a) Show the incomplete matching, M, that describes which present Granny had decided to give to each child.

(b) Use a matching algorithm to construct an alternating path for M in G, and hence find a maximal matching between the presents and the grandchildren.   (AQA)

5* A bipartite graph has the following adjacency matrix, where each non-zero entry corresponds to an edge.

$$\begin{array}{c} \\ A \\ B \\ C \\ D \end{array} \begin{array}{cccc} R & S & T & U \\ \left(0 \right. & 0 & 1 & \left. 0 \right) \\ 1 & 0 & 1 & 1 \\ 0 & 1 & 0 & 0 \\ \left(0 \right. & 1 & 1 & \left. 0 \right) \end{array}$$

(a) Find three lines which cover every non-zero entry.

(b) Find a matching of three pairs of vertices.

(c) What is the size of a maximum matching? Explain your answer.

6* The Matching Augmentation algorithm is applied to a bipartite graph for which the maximum matching has already been obtained. Explain why

(a) each edge of the bipartite graph either has an unlabelled left-vertex or a labelled right-vertex,

(b) all unlabelled left-vertices are in the matching,

(c) all labelled right-vertices are in the matching,

(d) each edge of the matching joins vertices which are either both labelled or both unlabelled.

6 Route inspection

This chapter looks at the problem of finding a closed trail covering every edge of a network. When you have completed it you should

- be aware of a wide range of route inspection problems
- be able to apply a standard method of solution to obtain the closed trail of minimum weight.

6.1 Traversability

Consider the task of a village police officer who must traverse each of the streets shown in Fig. 6.1.

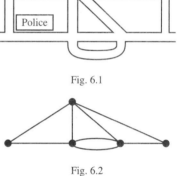

Fig. 6.1

Replacing roads by edges and junctions by vertices, you obtain the graph shown in Fig. 6.2.

Since each vertex has even order, the graph is Eulerian. The police officer can therefore choose a closed path which contains every edge precisely once, as shown in Fig. 6.3.

Fig. 6.2

The length of the police officer's route is then precisely the same as the length of all the streets, and that is clearly the best that can be achieved. However, for most networks of roads the situation will not be so simple.

Fig. 6.3

For example, consider Fig. 6.4.

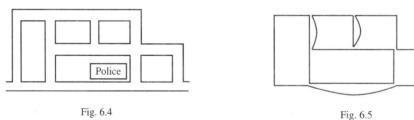

Fig. 6.4

Fig. 6.5

Here, the underlying graph has six vertices of odd order. The only way that a closed tour can traverse *every* edge is if some edges are repeated. For example, Fig. 6.5 shows that three edges are traversed twice.

The length of the police officer's route can now be thought of as

the length of all the streets + the lengths of repeated streets.

There are many practical situations which require the solution of a route inspection problem (that is, the finding of a closed tour containing every edge at least once). Situations similar to that of the police patrol are repairing track, delivering mail, seeding fields and clearing snow.

A modern application of route inspection is the checking of every link on a web site. Web sites can have hundreds of pages and thousands of links, and checking these links requires the involvement of both computers and humans. Computer software is used to check simple links and to keep track of the whole checking process, whereas human input is especially required for checking links which are more descriptive.

6.2 The Chinese Postman algorithm

You have seen that modern route inspection problems can involve large networks. There is therefore a need for a systematic procedure to obtain a closed trail containing every edge of minimum length, or weight.

The following well known procedure for finding the least-weight closed trail containing every edge (as required by a postman) was invented by a Chinese mathematician, Kuan Mei-Ko, in 1962.

Chinese Postman algorithm

Step 1   Find all vertices of odd order.

Step 2   For each pair of odd vertices find the connecting path of minimum weight.

Step 3   Pair up all the odd vertices so that the sum of the weights of the connecting paths from Step 2 is minimised.

Step 4   In the original graph, duplicate the minimum weight paths found in Step 3.

Step 5   Find a trail containing every edge for the new (Eulerian) graph.

Example 6.2.1

Find the minimum-weight closed trail containing all edges for the network in Fig. 6.6.

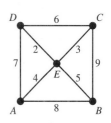

Fig. 6.6

The odd vertices are A, B, C and D (Step 1).

The minimum weights of the connecting paths are

$$AB\ 8, \quad BC\ 8, \quad AC\ 7, \quad BD\ 7, \quad AD\ 6, \quad CD\ 5 \text{ (Step 2)}.$$

The possible pairs, in which all the odd vertices are connected, are

$$AB, CD\ 8+5=13, \quad AC, BD\ 7+7=14, \quad AD, BC\ 6+8=14.$$

So the odd vertices should be paired up as AB and CD (Step 3).

Add in the edges *AB* and *CED* (Step 4).

Step 5 gives a trail of minimum weight: for example, *ABAEBCECDEDA*.

Its weight is

the length of all the streets + the lengths of repeated streets = $44 + 13 = 57$.

The Chinese Postman algorithm assumes that the original graph has an even number of vertices of odd order. This is actually true for *all* graphs. Note that each edge of a graph contributes 1 to the orders of two vertices, and so the sum of the orders of all the vertices is twice the number of edges. The number of vertices of odd order must therefore be even, as required. (See also Exercise 2B Question 7.)

When the number of vertices of odd order is relatively large, it can be very time-consuming to check all the possibilities, as in the next example.

Example 6.2.2
The network given in Fig. 6.7 gives the times (in minutes) it takes to drive along a number of streets in central London.

(a) List the vertices of odd order.

(b) Draw up a table showing the least times between the vertices of odd order.

(c) What would be the minimum time needed to complete a closed trail of every one of these streets? Write down such a closed trail.

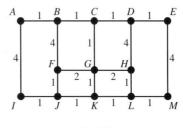

Fig. 6.7

(a) *B, C, D, F, H, J, K, L.*

(b)

	B	C	D	F	H	J	K	L
B	–	1	2	4	4	4	3	4
C	1	–	1	3	3	3	2	3
D	2	1	–	4	4	4	3	4
F	4	3	4	–	4	1	2	3
H	4	3	4	4	–	3	2	1
J	4	3	4	1	3	–	1	2
K	3	2	3	2	2	1	–	1
L	4	3	4	3	1	2	1	–

(c) The total weight of all streets is 32.

For Step 3, one good possibility for pairing off the vertices is

BD, CK, FJ, HL.

These paths have total length $2 + 2 + 1 + 1 = 6$.

For this to be beaten or even equalled, no edge of length 4 can be used, since $1 + 1 + 1 + 4 > 6$. Thus the extra path from B *must* start BC and the extra path from D *must* start DC. It should now be clear that the extra 6 minutes cannot be beaten and so the minimum time is $32 + 6 = 38$ minutes. An example of a minimum time trail is

AIJFJ KLHLM EDHGF BCDCG KGCBA.

Exercise 6A

1 A person delivering leaflets has to walk along each of the roads shown on the map. All the measurements are metres, and, except for at the crescent, all the angles are right angles.

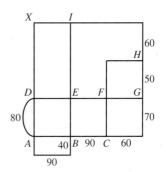

(a) Explain the relevance of those intersections where an odd number of roads meet.

(b) Find the shortest possible distance the person has to walk, starting and finishing at X. Show the results of each possible pairing of odd vertices.

(c) For each of the nine road intersections, find the number of times that the delivery person will pass through that intersection.

(d) What is the shortest possible distance the delivery person would have to walk if they started and finished at C? Explain your answer.

2 (In this question ignore the widths of the roads.)

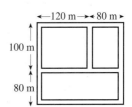

(a) Model this road system as a network in an appropriate way for

(i)   a delivery man who only needs to walk along each road once,

(ii) a postwoman who walks along both sides of each road,

(iii) a street cleaner who travels along both sides of each road in the correct direction.

(b) What is the total length of the roads in the network?

(c) In each case considered in part (a), find the total distance that will need to be travelled.

3 An electronic game takes place in an arena consisting of a 4×4 block of connected rooms.

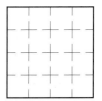

To complete the game, it is necessary to travel through each of the 24 doorways. Convert this problem into a route inspection problem, and find the least number of doorways that will have to be gone through twice.

4[*] (a) Consider the problem in Question 3, but with an $n \times n$ block of rooms, where n is even. The rooms are connected as in Question 3. Copy and complete the table.

Order	2	3	4
Number of vertices with that order			

How many edges (doorways) will need to be repeated?

(b) How many edges must be repeated if n is odd?

6.3   Pairing odd vertices

You have seen that the version of the Chinese Postman algorithm given in this chapter depends upon your performing the following operations.

* Consider all possible pairings of the vertices of odd order.
* Find the shortest distance between each pair of vertices of odd order.

The second of these can be performed by Dijkstra's algorithm, which has quadratic order. The important question, therefore, is how many times must this algorithm be performed, that is, how many pairings are there of the vertices of odd order.

For two odd vertices A and B, the only edge is AB, so there is 1 pairing.

For four odd vertices, A, B, C and D, the possible choices are AB with CD, AC with BD and AD with BC, so there are 3 pairings.

For six odd vertices, A, B, C, D, E and F,

> you can choose AB along with each of the three pairings of C, D, E and F;
> you can choose AC along with each of the three pairings of B, D, E and F;
> you can choose AD along with each of the three pairings of B, C, E and F;
> you can choose AE along with each of the three pairings of B, C, D and F;
> you can choose AF along with each of the three pairings of B, C, D and E.

There are therefore 15 pairings in total.

Table 6.8 shows the results for various numbers of vertices of odd order.

Number of odd vertices	Number of ways of pairing
2	1
4	3
6	15
8	105
10	945
12	10 395
14	135 135

Table 6.8

For more than six vertices of odd order it is clearly impractical to apply the Chinese Postman algorithm by hand. Even using a computer is problematical if the number of odd vertices is large, because the number of pairings is so large.

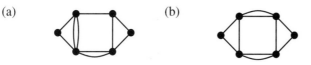

Exercise 6B

1 A child's toy consists of a number of pegs around which elastic bands are wrapped.

(a)   (b)

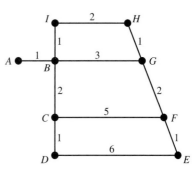

Which of (a) and (b) can be made with a single, continuous elastic band? Explain your answer.

2 A snow-plough must drive along all the main roads shown, starting and finishing at the garage at A. The distances in kilometres are marked.

(a) Explain why 25 km is a lower bound for the distance the snow-plough must travel.

(b) Find the least distance it must actually travel, showing your method clearly.

3 The matrix form for a weighted graph is shown in the table below.

	A	B	C	D	E	F	G	H
A	–	23	17	–	18	–	15	–
B	23	–	9	10	12	16	–	14
C	17	9	–	9	20	–	27	–
D	–	10	9	–	–	–	–	16
E	18	12	20	–	–	7	20	–
F	–	16	–	–	7	–	24	17
G	15	–	27	–	20	24	–	–
H	–	14	–	16	–	17	–	–

(a) Use Dijkstra's algorithm to find the shortest paths from H to C, D and E.

(b) Draw a weighted graph with vertices C, D, E, H and with each edge having the weight of the corresponding shortest path.

(c) Apply the Chinese Postman algorithm to the original network. Which edges should be duplicated?

4 (a) Look at Table 6.8. Why is the number of ways of pairing 8 vertices of odd order 105?

(b) Find a general formula for the other results in Table 6.8.

5 The following table of distances (in metres) between features in the gardens of a stately home was considered in Miscellaneous exercise 3.

	A	B	C	D	E	F	G
A	–	250	200	–	500	300	–
B	250	–	400	200	–	70	–
C	200	400	–	300	400	–	300
D	–	200	300	–	–	–	350
E	500	–	400	–	–	–	500
F	300	70	–	–	–	–	–
G	–	–	300	350	500	–	–

(a) What is the total length of all the paths?

(b) What distance must be covered if each path is to be inspected?

6 Apply the Chinese Postman algorithm to the network of distances, in kilometres, shown below. Which roads should be repeated?

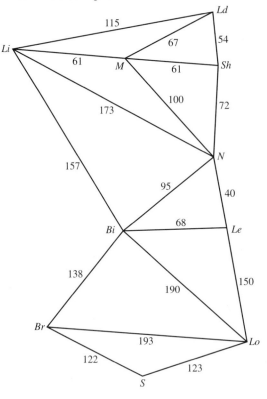

7 A network of pipelines is as shown, with distances in metres. A fault has to be located. What is the shortest route which will cover every length of pipeline at least once? Show your method fully.

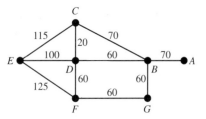

Miscellaneous exercise 6

1 A steam railway connects four stations, as shown in the figure.

Ann O'Rak, a steam railway enthusiast, wants to travel every section of track, starting and finishing at A.

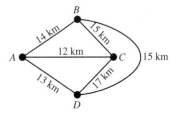

(a) Explain why it will be necessary for Ann to travel some sections of track twice. Write down the minimum number of tracks that will have to be repeated.

(b) By considering all pairings, find the minimum distance that Ann must travel to cover every section of track, starting and finishing at A. Give a possible route that she could take.

(c) Suppose that the railway had connected five stations, with every station connected to every other station. How many pairings would need to be considered to solve Ann's problem? (OCR)

2 (a) Explain why the number of odd vertices in any graph is always an even number.

The network in the figure represents the paths in a woodland park; the distances are in hundreds of metres.

The members of a family have been walking in the woods. When they get back to the car park they find that their youngest child has lost his teddy bear somewhere on the walk. They do not know which paths they have used, so the father decides to go back and cover every path in the woods.

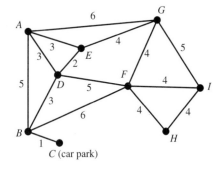

(b) By considering all possible pairings of odd vertices, find the length of the shortest route that the father can take to cover every path in the woods. You should explain your method carefully. (OCR)

3 The figure shows the bipartite graph $K_{3,3}$, in which each of the three vertices A, B and C are joined to each of the three vertices X, Y and Z using the nine edges shown.

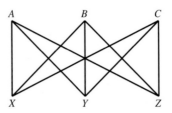

The table gives the length, in kilometres, of each edge.

	X	Y	Z
A	2	3	4
B	15	11	12
C	6	5	9

Consider the route inspection problem of finding the length of the shortest route that starts and finishes at A, and travels each edge at least once. The method to be used is to check all the possible pairings between the vertices on one side of the bipartite graph and the vertices on the other side of the bipartite graph.

(a) Apply the method to the graph shown in the figure.

(b) Show that using the method on the graph $K_{3,3}$ requires $(2 \times 6) + 8 + 1 = 21$ additions.

In the bipartite graph $K_{5,5}$, each of the five vertices A, B, C, D and E is joined to each of the five vertices, V, W, X, Y and Z using twenty-five edges.

(c) Show that using the method on the graph $K_{5,5}$ requires $(4 \times 120) + 24 + 1 = 505$ additions.

(d) Calculate the number of additions needed when using the method on $K_{n,n}$ where n is an odd positive integer.   (OCR, adapted)

4 A highways department has to inspect its roads for fallen trees.

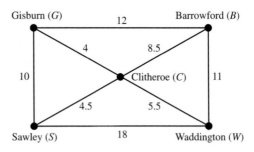

(a) The diagram shows the lengths of the roads, in miles, that have to be inspected in one district.

   (i) List the three different ways in which the four odd vertices in the diagram can be paired.

  (ii) Find the shortest distance that has to be travelled in inspecting all the roads in the district, starting and finishing at the same point.

(b) The connected graph of the roads in another district has six odd vertices. Find the number of ways of pairing these odd vertices.

(c) For a connected graph with n odd vertices, find an expression for the number of ways of pairing these odd vertices.   (AQA)

5 The edges of the network in the figure represent roads in a small housing estate. There is only one road in to and out of the estate, represented by edge AB. The lengths of the roads are shown in metres.

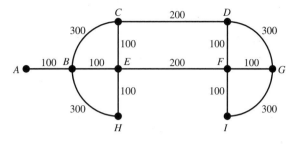

The total length of roads is 2300 m.

(a) A papergirl delivers to about 20% of the houses and therefore finds it worthwhile to cross from side to side of a road whilst making deliveries. Thus, she would prefer to walk along each road only once.

Use an appropriate algorithm to find the minimum total length of road along which she must walk if she starts and finishes her round at A. Indicate how you applied the algorithm.

(b) A postman delivers to about 80% of the houses. He finds it better to deliver to one side of a road at a time. He therefore needs to walk along each road at least twice. If he starts and finishes at A, find the minimum distance that he must walk, justifying your answer.

(c) Suppose that the postman acquires a bicycle. This means that he would still like to travel along each road twice, but in opposite directions, so that he is always riding on the correct side of the road. Will this mean that he must travel further? Justify your answer. (AQA)

6 A groundsman at a local sports centre has to mark out the lines of several five-a-side pitches using white paint. He is unsure as to the size of the goal area and he decides to paint the outline as given below, where all the distances given are in metres.

(a) He starts and finishes at the point A. Find the minimum total distance that he must walk and give one of the corresponding possible routes.

(b) Before he starts to paint the second pitch he is told that each goal area is a semicircle of radius 5 metres, as shown in the diagram below.

   (i) Find an optimal 'Chinese postman' route around the lines. Calculate the length of your route.

   (ii) State which vertices would be suitable starting points to keep to a minimum the total distance walked from when he starts to paint the lines until he completes the painting.

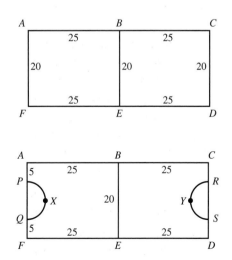

(AQA)

7 A road gritting service is based at a point A. It is responsible for gritting the network of
roads shown in the diagram, where the distances shown are in miles.

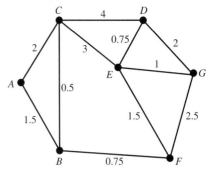

(a) Explain why it is not possible to start from
A and, by travelling along each road only
once, return to A.

(b) In the network there are four odd vertices,
B, D, F and G. List the different ways
in which these odd vertices can be
arranged as two pairs.

(c) For each pairing you have listed in part
(b), write down the sum of the shortest
distance between the first pair and the
shortest distance between the second pair.

(d) Hence find an optimal 'Chinese Postman' route around the network, starting and
finishing at A. State the length of your route.   (AQA)

8 (a) The network represents a road system in
which the lengths of the roads are shown
in kilometres. The road system has to be
cleared of snow by a snow-plough which is
based at A. The snow-plough only needs
to travel along each road once in order to
clear it. However, when all roads have
been cleared it must return to its base at A.

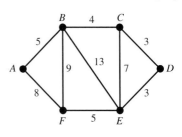

(i) State which roads the snow-plough should drive along twice in order to
travel the minimum total distance.

(ii) Hence solve the Chinese Postman problem for this network to find a route for the
snow-plough, starting and finishing at A.

(iii) The road BE becomes a dual carriageway and must be cleared twice, once in each
direction. Redraw the network to take account of this and find, by inspection, a
new route for the snow-plough.

(b) The original network has to be drawn as efficiently as possible by a pen operated by a
computer. Explain how this can be done without lifting the pen from the paper and
without tracing any of the edges more than once.   (AQA)

7 The travelling salesperson problem

This chapter is about finding a tour that visits every vertex of a network. When you have completed it you should

- appreciate that evaluating all tours is not practical for large scale problems
- be able to apply an algorithm to find a solution (not necessarily the best)
- know how to obtain bounds within which the best solution must lie.

7.1 The classical problem

You have seen that the problem of finding a tour that visits every edge (the route inspection problem) depended upon the earlier work of the mathematician Euler. Similarly, the problem of finding a tour visiting every vertex was studied in the 19th century by the Irish mathematician Sir William Hamilton.

A **Hamiltonian cycle** is defined to be a tour which contains every vertex precisely once. In a simple case, such as that of the network in Fig. 7.1, it is easy to list all the Hamiltonian cycles.

There are just three essentially different Hamiltonian cycles:

Fig. 7.1

     $ACBDA$ with weight 16,
     $ABCDA$ with weight 17,
     $ABDCA$ with weight 17.

Note, for example, that the cycle $ADBCA$ is just the first cycle reversed and so is not essentially different from it.

The classical travelling salesperson problem is to find the Hamiltonian cycle of minimum weight. In the above case this is the cycle $ACBDA$.

However, not all graphs have Hamiltonian cycles. For example, the network shown in Fig. 7.2 does not have any cycles passing through A.

Nevertheless, a salesperson living, say, in town B might still need to find the shortest round trip visiting every town. To enable you to use this chapter's methods for finding Hamiltonian cycles, you can replace any network like Fig. 7.2 by the complete network of shortest distances. The shortest distance between A and C is 33, via D. If you add the direct edge AC, of weight 33, you have not changed the

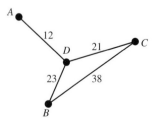

Fig. 7.2

problem. Adding all such edges, you get Fig. 7.3.

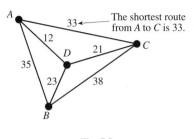

Fig. 7.3

For the remainder of this chapter it is therefore assumed that the problem is always the classical one of finding a Hamiltonian cycle of minimum weight, with no repetition of vertices.

7.2   A difficult problem

In Section 7.1 you saw how to find the minimum Hamiltonian cycle for a graph with four vertices by listing all three possible cycles.

Unfortunately, as the number of vertices increases, the number of possible Hamiltonian cycles tends to increase very rapidly. For graphs where all vertices are directly linked to each other, Table 7.4 shows the numbers of Hamiltonian cycles for small values of n.

Number of vertices, n	Number of Hamiltonian cycles
3	1
4	3
5	12
6	60
7	360

Table 7.4

To see how to calculate these numbers, consider the case $n = 5$ and suppose the vertices are A, B, C, D and E. Vertex A must be on each cycle, and so you may as well always start from A. There are then four possibilities for the next vertex, three for the one after, two for the one after that, and just one possibility for the final vertex before returning to A.

This gives $4 \times 3 \times 2 \times 1 = 24$ sequences. However, each Hamiltonian cycle corresponds to two sequences, since, for example, $ABCDEA$ and its reverse $AEDCBA$ are taken to be the same Hamiltonian cycle. So if $n = 5$, there are $\frac{1}{2} \times 24$, or 12, Hamiltonian cycles.

In general, for n vertices, the number of Hamiltonian cycles is

$$\tfrac{1}{2} \times (n-1) \times (n-2) \times \ldots \times 3 \times 2 \times 1 = \tfrac{1}{2}(n-1)!$$

The symbol $n!$, called 'factorial n', denotes $n \times (n-1) \times (n-2) \times \ldots \times 3 \times 2 \times 1$.

The method of evaluating all Hamiltonian cycles therefore requires consideration of $\frac{1}{2}(n-1)!$ cycles. To see what this means for computer time, consider a 600 MHz processor (that is, one capable of performing 600 million simple operations per second). If there were 20 vertices, there would be $\frac{1}{2} \times 19!$, or 6×10^{16}, Hamiltonian cycles. Even with the assumption that the computer could check an entire tour in a single operation, a problem with just 20 vertices would require about 10^8 seconds, which is about 3 years, of computer time!

All methods discovered to date for solving the travelling salesperson problem are very time consuming and so attention has been focused on finding not the optimal solution, but simply a reasonably good solution.

7.3   The Nearest Neighbour algorithm

A simple way of trying to find a reasonably good Hamiltonian cycle is to try a greedy algorithm, such as the Nearest Neighbour algorithm. At each stage it visits the nearest vertex which has not already been visited.

The Nearest Neighbour algorithm

Step 1   Choose any starting vertex.

Step 2   Consider the edges which join the previously chosen vertex to not-yet-chosen vertices. From these edges pick one that has minimum weight. Choose this edge, and the new vertex on the end of it, to join the cycle.

Step 3   Repeat Step 2 until all vertices have been chosen.

Step 4   Then add the edge that joins the last-chosen vertex to the first-chosen vertex.

Example 7.3.1

A small chemical plant can be used to produce any one of five chemicals, A, B, C, D and E. The times (in hours) required for cleaning the equipment, and setting it up again for making the next chemical, are as shown in Fig. 7.5. Use the Nearest Neighbour algorithm to find a small total changeover time for production of all five chemicals, starting and finishing with chemical A.

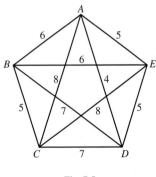

Fig. 7.5

Starting from A, the first edge is AD, as 4 is the least of 6, 8, 4 and 5.

From D, DE is chosen as 5 is the least of 7, 7 and 5.

This is followed by EB, with weight 6 as the lesser of 6 and 8.

Finally, you are forced to choose BC and CA.

The cycle is $ADEBCA$, which has weight 28 hours.

The Nearest Neighbour algorithm is 'greedy' because at each stage the immediately best route is chosen, without a look ahead to possible future problems. The next example shows how this greed can sometimes lead to a poor solution.

Example 7.3.2
A warehouse in Toulouse supplies goods to retail outlets in Bordeaux, Calais, Dijon, Lyons, Marseille, Orléans, Poitiers and St-Etienne. The distances involved (in kilometres) are shown in Fig. 7.6. Use the Nearest Neighbour algorithm, starting from Toulouse, to find a single delivery route to all the towns.

```
Bordeaux
870    Calais
641    543    Dijon
550    751    192    Lyons
649    1067   507    316    Marseille
457    421    297    445    761    Orléans
247    625    515    431    733    212    Poitiers
519    803    244    59     309    392    421    St-Etienne
244    996    726    535    405    582    435    528    Toulouse
```

Fig. 7.6

The solution is

Toulouse $\xrightarrow{244}$ Bordeaux $\xrightarrow{247}$ Poitiers $\xrightarrow{212}$ Orleans $\xrightarrow{297}$ Dijon

$\downarrow 192$

Toulouse $\xleftarrow{996}$ Calais $\xleftarrow{1067}$ Marseille $\xleftarrow{309}$ St-Etienne $\xleftarrow{59}$ Lyons

You should notice that because it was greedy early on, the tour has had to include two extremely large distances at the end. A glance at a map of France shows that Calais should have been included somewhere near the Poitiers–Orléans–Dijon stretch of the tour. Sometimes, a different choice of initial vertex avoids this type of problem (see Exercise 7A Question 2).

Another possible problem with the Nearest Neighbour algorithm is that it may lead to an incomplete tour, as you will see in the next example.

Example 7.3.3
A holidaymaker on Guernsey hires a bicycle at St Peter Port and wants to complete a tour of the nine places marked on the map of Fig. 7.7. What happens if the Nearest Neighbour algorithm is applied, starting at St Peter Port?

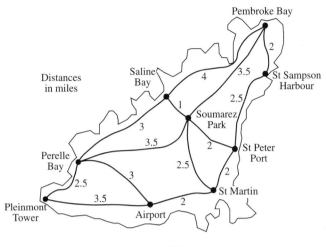

Fig. 7.7

Depending upon the first choice of edge from St Peter Port, the algorithm starts by giving either

St Peter Port–Soumarez Park–Saline Bay–...

or

St Peter Port–St Martin–Airport–Perelle Bay–... .

In both cases, you have crossed from one side of the island to the other. If you now go south, you cannot complete the tour by visiting the places in the north without re-visiting one of the places on the route which crosses the island. Similarly, if you go north, you also have to re-visit one of the places on the route which crosses the island to get to the south of the island.

In conclusion, you should treat the Nearest Neighbour algorithm as only a rough and ready attempt to obtain a good tour. Do not worry about the fact that it does not always lead to a good solution.

Exercise 7

1 (a) List the three possible Hamiltonian cycles for the network of Fig. 7.3.

   (b) What route should the salesperson take for the network shown in Fig. 7.2?

2 Apply the Nearest Neighbour algorithm to the problem of Example 7.3.2, but this time starting from Calais.

3 Delete the road from Perelle Bay to the Airport on the map given in Fig. 7.7. Show how the Nearest Neighbour algorithm, starting at Pembroke Bay, can now lead to a Hamiltonian cycle for this network. What is its length?

4   A delivery firm's costs (in £) for travelling between five towns are as shown in the table.

	A	B	C	D	E
A	–	60	50	40	70
B	60	–	90	–	80
C	50	90	–	80	–
D	40	–	80	–	90
E	70	80	–	90	–

(a) Find the cost for a round trip through all the towns by using the Nearest Neighbour algorithm starting from A .

(b) Find an improved route by using the Nearest Neighbour algorithm starting from a different town.

(c) From which town does the Nearest Neighbour algorithm not work?

7.4   A lower bound

You have seen that even when the Nearest Neighbour algorithm does lead to a Hamiltonian cycle, this may well not have the minimum possible weight. How, therefore, do you know whether a cycle that you have found is close to being the best possible, or whether you should continue searching for a much better one? Fortunately, there is a clever method for showing that there is a limit to how low the total weight of a Hamiltonian cycle can be.

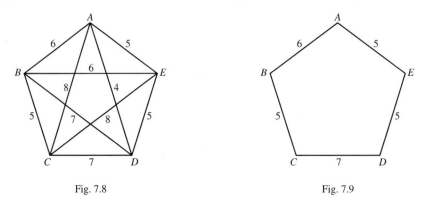

Fig. 7.8   Fig. 7.9

In Example 7.3.1, a Hamiltonian cycle of total weight 28 was found for the network shown in Fig. 7.8. Consider this Hamiltonian cycle as drawn in Fig. 7.9.

You should be able to see that *any* Hamiltonian cycle for the original network will consist of

* two edges from vertex A , and
* three edges linking the points B , C , D and E .

Note that the two edges from vertex A must have a total weight at least $4 + 5$ (taking the two smallest weights of edges incident at A). Furthermore, by applying Prim's algorithm to the network on just the points B , C , D and E , you can see that the three edges linking the points B , C , D and E must have total weight at least $5 + 5 + 6$ (the weight of a minimum connector on B , C , D and E).

So it is *impossible* for any Hamiltonian cycle to have total weight less than $4+5+5+5+6 = 25$.

You now know that the minimum possible weight for a Hamiltonian cycle for this network lies between 25 hours and the value found in Example 7.3.1, 28 hours.

The upper bound of 28 hours was obtained by simply finding a tour with that weight. The lower bound of 25 hours was found by considering the network on B, C, D and E separately from the edges incident at A.

Either by finding a different tour or by splitting the network up differently, or both, it may be possible to further 'improve' these bounds. That is, it may be possible to narrow the range within which the weight of the minimum Hamiltonian cycle must lie.

The method for finding a lower bound can be described in general as an algorithm.

The Lower Bound algorithm

Step 1   Choose an arbitrary vertex, say X. Find the total of the two smallest weights of edges incident at X.

Step 2   Consider the network obtained by ignoring X and all edges incident to X. Find the total weight of the minimum connector for this network.

Step 3   The sum of the two totals is a lower bound.

Example 7.4.1
Consider the network shown in Fig. 7.8.
(a) Apply the Nearest Neighbour algorithm starting from B.
(b) Apply the Lower Bound algorithm with C as the special vertex.
(c) What can you say about the minimum Hamiltonian cycle?

(a) The algorithm gives $B \xrightarrow{5} C \xrightarrow{7} D \xrightarrow{4} A \xrightarrow{5} E \xrightarrow{6} B$, with weight 27.

(b) For C, the sum of the two smallest edges is $5+7 = 12$.

For the remainder, the minimum connector is $4+5+6 = 15$.

The total is therefore $12+15 = 27$.

(c) The solutions to (a) and (b) show that $27 \leqslant$ minimal weight $\leqslant 27$. So in this case the Nearest Neighbour algorithm has found the minimum Hamiltonian cycle.

7.5   Tour improvement

In cases where there is a large gap between the upper and lower bounds for a tour, it may be worth trying to improve the best tour obtained so far, rather than looking for a completely different tour. A number of algorithms have been developed to attempt this improvement. In this section you will learn one such method.

Consider, for example, the network shown in
Fig. 7.10 with the weight on each edge being the
distance on the page between the two points.

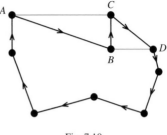

Applying the Nearest Neighbour algorithm from
the vertex B would lead to the tour shown in
Fig. 7.10. However, the part of the tour $ABCD$
can be replaced by $ACBD$. This gives a reduction
in distance, because

Fig. 7.10

$$d(A,C) + d(B,D) < d(A,B) + d(C,D),$$

where $d(V,W)$ means the weight of the edge between vertices V and W.

You can use this idea as the basis for a general attempt to improve tours. Let V_1, V_2, ... , V_n
be the successive vertices of a Hamiltonian tour, and let $V_{n+1} = V_1$, $V_{n+2} = V_2$ and $V_{n+3} = V_3$.

Tour Improvement algorithm

Step 1   Let $i = 1$.

Step 2   If $d(V_i, V_{i+2}) + d(V_{i+1}, V_{i+3}) < d(V_i, V_{i+1}) + d(V_{i+2}, V_{i+3})$, then swap
V_{i+1} and V_{i+2}.

Step 3   Replace i by $i+1$.

Step 4   If $i \leq n$ then go back to Step 2.

To apply an algorithm such as this one to a large tour may be time-consuming.
However, it can easily be programmed for a computer.

When using a computer program to improve tours it can be useful to start with an initial tour,
even a very inefficient one. One possibility is to travel along each edge of a minimum
connector twice, as in the next example. Note that this will give you a closed trail but not a
cycle; a Hamiltonian cycle can then be obtained by finding short-cuts.

Example 7.5.1
Consider the network in Fig. 7.11, which is a
copy of Fig. 7.1.

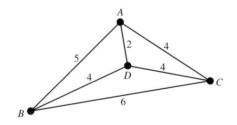

(a) Find a minimum connector, and hence find
a closed trail containing all the vertices with
total weight twice that of the minimum
connector.

Fig. 7.11

(b) Obtain a Hamiltonian cycle by finding
short-cuts, and then apply the Tour
Improvement algorithm to obtain a tour of weight 16.

(a) Fig. 7.12 shows a minimum connector, and Fig. 7.13 shows a closed trail *ADCDBDA* whose weight is twice that of the minimum connector.

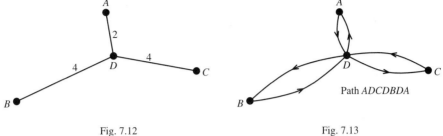

Fig. 7.12   Fig. 7.13

(b) The tour can be reduced by going from *A* to *C* directly instead of via *D*, and by going from *B* to *A* directly instead of via *D*. The tour is then *ACDBA*, of weight 17.

When you do Step 2 of the Tour Improvement algorithm with $i = 2$, you find that

$$\text{weight}(CB) + \text{weight}(DA) = 6 + 2 = 8,$$

whereas

$$\text{weight}(CD) + \text{weight}(BA) = 4 + 5 = 9.$$

So swap *D* and *B*. This gives the better cycle *ACBDA*, with weight 16.

Miscellaneous exercise 7

1 Consider the travelling salesperson problem for the network in the diagram.

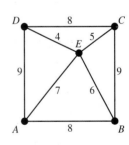

(a) Apply the Lower Bound algorithm with *A*, *B*, *C* or *D* as the special vertex. What do you notice?

(b) Apply the Lower Bound algorithm with *E* as the special vertex.

(c) Explain why the bound of part (b) cannot be attained.

(d) What is the optimum solution?

2 The distances shown on the network are in kilometres.

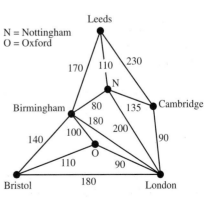

(a) Apply the Nearest Neighbour algorithm from Birmingham.

(b) Improve the tour of part (a) by using the Tour Improvement algorithm.

(c) Apply the Lower Bound algorithm with Leeds as the special vertex. What can you now say about the optimum solution to the travelling salesperson problem for this network?

3 A firm uses certain specified routes between the following cities for its deliveries. The distances are in miles.

	Bi	Br	Ld	Le	Li	Lo	M	N	Sh	So
Birmingham	–	138	–	68	157	190	–	95	–	–
Bristol	138	–	–	–	–	193	–	–	–	122
Leeds	–	–	–	–	115	–	67	–	54	–
Leicester	68	–	–	–	–	150	–	40	–	–
Liverpool	157	–	115	–	–	–	61	173	–	–
London	190	193	–	150	–	–	–	–	–	123
Manchester	–	–	67	–	61	–	–	100	61	–
Nottingham	95	–	–	40	173	–	100	–	72	–
Sheffield	–	–	54	–	–	–	61	72	–	–
Southampton	–	122	–	–	–	123	–	–	–	–

(a) Apply the Nearest Neighbour algorithm starting from Leicester.

(b) Find the weight of a minimum spanning tree for the network with Southampton deleted.

(c) Make a deduction about the optimum solution to the travelling salesperson problem.

4 Draw three simple networks, with Hamiltonian paths, such that the optimum solutions to the Travelling Salesperson problem have weights

(a) less than twice,   (b) exactly twice,   (c) more than twice

the weight of the minimum connector.

5 A ring main consists of a loop of cable running from the electricity meter M to five double sockets in turn and then back to the meter. The estimated cost of each possible stretch of cable is as shown in the table.

	M	A	B	C	D	E
M	–	13	14	13	16	12
A	13	–	12	–	–	11
B	14	12	–	16	–	–
C	13	–	16	–	14	–
D	16	–	–	14	–	13
E	12	11	–	–	13	–

(a) Apply the Nearest Neighbour algorithm from M, then A, and finally E.

(b) Apply the Lower Bound algorithm from M. What can you deduce about the least cost of laying the ring main cable?

(c) Fitting each double socket costs £25. What effect does this have on the optimum path for laying the cable?

6 A modification of the Nearest Neighbour algorithm for use with the *practical* travelling salesperson problem is as follows.

Step 1 Choose any starting vertex.

Step 2 Choose a vertex which is at a minimal distance from the previously chosen mode.

Step 3 Repeat Step 2 until all vertices have been chosen.

Apply this algorithm to Question 5(a), starting from A.

7 An assembly line is used to produce five items, A, B, C, D and E. The times (in minutes) needed for each possible changeover are shown in the table.

	To A	B	C	D	E
From A	–	30	50	70	40
B	20	–	30	80	50
C	60	50	–	20	30
D	40	70	40	–	40
E	80	20	30	40	–

All five items need to be produced, and the assembly line must be returned to its initial state. The factory manager wishes to minimise the changeover time.

(a) What is the result of applying the Nearest Neighbour algorithm from A?

(b) Apply the Lower Bound algorithm with A as the special vertex.

(c) Improve the upper bound of part (a).

8 Find a Hamiltonian cycle in this graph of the dodecahedron. (This was the problem initially considered by Hamilton.)

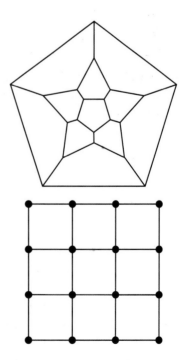

9 Find a Hamiltonian cycle for all $n \times n$ rectangular arrays of vertices with n even. The case $n = 4$ is illustrated.

10* Prove that an $n \times n$ rectangular array of vertices, with n odd, cannot have a Hamiltonian cycle.

11 Pirate Pete is hunting for buried treasure. He knows that the treasure is buried at one of the places marked on his map, shown in the figure, but he cannot solve the clues to find out where he should dig.

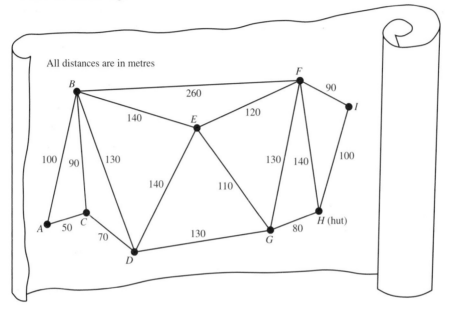

Pirate Pete decides to dig at each of the places marked on his map.

(a) Demonstrate, clearly, the use of a greedy algorithm, starting from the hut, H, to construct a minimum spanning tree (minimum connector) for the network.

(b) Explain, briefly, why twice the length of the minimum spanning tree gives an upper bound to the length of the route which is the solution to the practical travelling salesperson problem for the network.

(c) Write down a route that gives a better upper bound than that found in part (b), and state the length of this route.   (OCR)

12 A travelling salesman wishes to visit each of eight towns, returning to the town where he started.

The diagram shows the distances, in miles, between the eight towns.

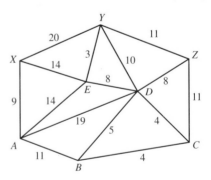

(a) Find a minimum spanning tree for the eight towns, stating its length.

(b) Use your answer to part (a) to find an upper bound for a tour of the eight towns.

(c) Use the nearest neighbour algorithm to find an improved upper bound starting from town Z.

(d) By deleting town X obtain a lower bound for a tour.

(e) Hence write down inequalities for L, the minimum length of a tour of the eight towns.

(AQA, adapted)

13 A machine is used for producing ice cream in six flavours. The machine produces one flavour of ice cream at a time. It needs to be cleaned before changing flavours. The times taken to clean the machine depend on the two flavours involved and these times, in minutes, are given in the table. The machine is set to produce each flavour in sequence before repeating the cycle. The machine can start the cycle with any flavour.

From \ To	Vanilla	Lemon	Orange	Raspberry	Coffee	Mint
Vanilla	—	40	35	35	42	40
Lemon	30	—	25	26	30	45
Orange	20	45	—	30	35	34
Raspberry	35	40	30	—	40	25
Coffee	25	35	22	30	—	30
Mint	30	40	34	25	35	—

(a) Upper bound times in excess of three hours are produced by using the nearest neighbour algorithm when starting with Vanilla or Raspberry. Use the same method to find four further upper bounds for the total cleaning time, showing that only one produces a total time of under 175 minutes.

The manager of the factory realises that he must select one number from each row and one number from each column to represent a complete cycle.

Hence from Vanilla the time must be at least 35 minutes, and one of 5, 0, 0, 7 or 5 minutes must be added to this time. So from Vanilla to Coffee the time is 35 minutes plus an adjusted time of 7 minutes.

(b) Repeat this procedure for each other flavour stating the minimum time from each row, and hence produce a matrix of adjusted times.

(c) One number must be selected from each column of the adjusted times. Find the minimum adjusted time for each column, and produce a new matrix of times which allows for both the minimum row and the minimum column.

(d) Hence state a lower bound for the time for the complete cleaning cycle and find a cycle that will produce a total cleaning time of under 170 minutes. (AQA)

8 Linear programming

In this chapter you will learn how to tackle a range of maximising and minimising problems subject to various conditions or constraints. When you have completed it you should

- know what objective functions and linear constraints are
- be able to formulate practical problems as linear programming problems
- be able to solve linear programming problems by graphical means.

8.1 Optimisation

In an optimisation problem, the objective is to optimise (maximise or minimise) some function. Typical problems from the world of business might include

- maximising profits
- minimising costs
- maximising turnover
- minimising the time needed
- maximising the number of customers.

The following example is somewhat simplified, but it gives you an idea of the kind of situation which can arise.

As an example of a linear programming problem and its formulation as a problem, consider a recycling plant which produces two types of paper, P_1 and P_2, by using a mixture of scrap paper and timber.

Each tonne of paper P_1 requires 2 tonnes of scrap paper, and each tonne of paper P_2 requires 1 tonne of scrap paper, and there is a maximum of 16 tonnes of scrap paper available.

In addition, each tonne of paper P_1 requires 2 tonnes of timber, and each tonne of paper P_2 requires 3 tonnes of timber, and there is a maximum of 24 tonnes of timber available.

How can the plant maximise the total amount of paper produced per day?

You may find it helpful to summarise the information in a table like Table 8.1.

Raw material	Raw material per tonne of paper		Availability per day
	P_1	P_2	
Scrap paper	2 tonnes	1 tonne	16 tonnes
Timber	2 tonnes	3 tonnes	24 tonnes

Table 8.1

First you need to define the variables in terms of which the problem can be formulated. In this case, suppose the plant produces x tonnes of P_1 and y tonnes of P_2 each day.

As x tonnes of P_1 and y tonnes of P_2 requires $2x + y$ tonnes of scrap paper, and, as only 16 tonnes are available, $2x + y \leqslant 16$.

Similarly x tonnes of P_1 and y tonnes of P_2 requires $2x + 3y$ tonnes of timber, and only 24 tonnes are available. Therefore $2x + 3y \leqslant 24$.

In addition, you cannot produce negative amounts of P_1 and P_2, so $x \geqslant 0$ and $y \geqslant 0$.

The inequalities $x \geqslant 0$ and $y \geqslant 0$ are likely to be part of every problem like this.

The total amount of paper produced per day, which has to be maximised, is $x + y$.

Summarising this,

maximise $x + y$,

subject to $2x + y \leqslant 16$,   (scrap paper)
                  $2x + 3y \leqslant 24$,   (timber)
                         $x \geqslant 0$,
                         $y \geqslant 0$.

Now that the problem has been stated, it is time to take stock with some definitions.

The variables x and y used to formulate the problem are called **control variables**. The function to be optimised is called the **objective function**. The inequalities are examples of **constraints**; for reasons which will become clear later, they are called 'linear' constraints. So, in this problem you have to maximise the objective function $x + y$ subject to the four linear constraints.

The solution to the problem will be continued in Section 8.3, after some important graphical ideas in Section 8.2. You may wish to think about its solution before going further.

8.2   Representing inequalities graphically

You can visualise an inequality such as $a > b$ by saying that a lies to the right of b on a number line (see Fig. 8.2).

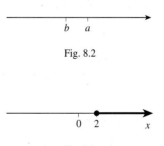

Fig. 8.2

You can describe the inequality $x \geqslant 2$ by saying it is satisfied by all the points on the number line which lie to the right of the point 2, or at the point 2 itself. It can be represented by a diagram such as Fig. 8.3, where the solid blob shows that the point $x = 2$ is included.

Fig. 8.3

Now look at the inequality $y \geqslant x+1$. You know that $y = x+1$ is the equation of a line, and that $y = x+1$ is also a rule for determining whether or not a given point in the plane with coordinates (x, y) lies on the line. Fig. 8.4 shows the graph of $y = x+1$.

If the equation is not satisfied by a given point, then the point does not lie on the line, so it is either above the line or below the line.

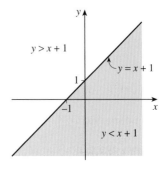

For such a point $y \neq x+1$, so either $y > x+1$ or $y < x+1$. The points which satisfy $y > x+1$ or $y < x+1$ are the points which are not on the line.

Points above the line (the unshaded region) have coordinates (x, y) which satisfy $y > x+1$. The points below the line satisfy $y < x+1$. For example, the point $(2, 4)$ has the property that $y > x+1$, and it is clearly above the line.

Fig. 8.4

In general, the line $y = mx + c$ divides the plane into three regions.

- The points on the line satisfy $y = mx + c$.
- Points in the region above the line satisfy $y > mx + c$.
- Points in the region below the line satisfy $y < mx + c$.

The inequality $y \geqslant x+1$ consists of the points which satisfy the line $y = x+1$ and the inequality $y > x+1$. It therefore consists of the line in Fig. 8.4, together with the unshaded points above the line.

Note that to illustrate $y > x+1$ it is conventional to draw $y = x+1$ as a dotted or dashed line, and to shade the region you do not require.

Example 8.2.1
Draw diagrams to show the regions satisfied by the inequalities
(a) $y \geqslant x$,   (b) $2x + y \leqslant 2$,   (c) $x \geqslant 0$,   (d) $x - 2y \leqslant 1$.
In each case, shade the unwanted region.

The diagrams are shown in Fig. 8.5, after the commentary.

(a) Draw the line $y = x$. Then the required region consists of the points on the line, and the points which lie above the line. Notice that the shading is on the other side of the line, and rules out the points which do *not* satisfy the inequality. It is conventional to indicate the required region by shading in this way; it is also usual not to shade out the whole of the unwanted region, as otherwise these diagrams tend to become messy.

(b) Since you can write $2x + y \leqslant 2$ in the form $y \leqslant 2 - 2x$, you can now use the method in the shaded box.

(c) Strictly, the shaded box does not apply to inequalities of this type, but it is easy to see that $x \geqslant 0$ corresponds to the region to the right of $x = 0$.

(d) You need to take some care with this because of the sign of y. Since $x - 2y \leqslant 1$, $x - 1 \leqslant 2y$, so $y \geqslant \frac{1}{2}x - \frac{1}{2}$.

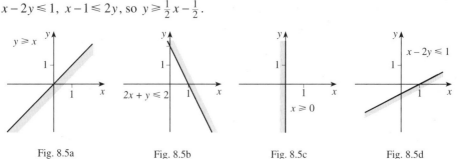

Fig. 8.5a   Fig. 8.5b   Fig. 8.5c   Fig. 8.5d

Example 8.2.2

Indicate by shading the region whose points satisfy the constraints $y \geqslant x$, $2x + y \leqslant 2$, $x \geqslant 0$ and $x - 2y \leqslant 1$. Use your diagram to find the coordinates of the point in the region which has the greatest x-coordinate.

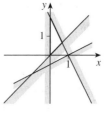

These constraints are just the ones of Example 8.2.1. So put the diagrams in Fig. 8.5 together, as in Fig. 8.6. The required region is the small triangle with no shading in it. The point with the greatest x-coordinate is found to be $\left(\frac{2}{3}, \frac{2}{3}\right)$ by solving the simultaneous equations $2x + y = 2$ and $x = y$.

Fig. 8.6

Notice that the constraint $x - 2y \leqslant 1$ plays no part in determining the region that satisfies all four constraints.

If in this example you had shaded the wanted regions, then the required region (the small triangle) would have been shaded four times, and it would be harder to pick out.

Notice also that in Example 8.2.2, you were effectively asked to maximise the value of x over all the points in that region. The maximum value of x turned out to be $\frac{2}{3}$.

Now suppose that you had been asked to maximise the value of $x + y$ in the triangular region not shaded in Fig. 8.6. In Fig. 8.7 you will see a magnified version of this region and a number of parallel lines, all of the form $x + y = k$ for various values of k. The value of k for each line is shown either at the bottom of the graph or along the right side.

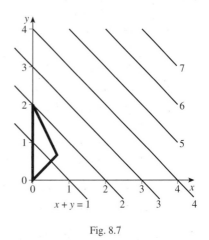

The important thing to notice is that the value of k increases as the parallel lines move to the right. The maximum value of $x + y$ for the region is the line furthest to the right which passes through a point of the region. This is the line which passes through $(0, 2)$, giving $x + y$ equal to $2 + 0 = 2$.

Fig. 8.7

Example 8.2.3

Maximise $2x + y$ subject to the constraints $3x + y \leqslant 6$, $x + 2y \leqslant 7$, $x \geqslant 0$ and $y \geqslant 0$.

Fig. 8.8 shows the region which satisfies the four constraints. In addition, a line parallel to the family of lines $2x + y = k$ has been drawn. As k increases, these parallel lines get further to the right (and as it decreases they get further left), so the maximum value of $2x + y$ arises when the line passes through the marked point, which has coordinates $(1, 3)$. This maximum value is then $2 \times 1 + 3 = 5$.

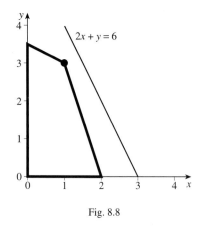

Fig. 8.8

Note that you find graphically which point gives the maximum, and then calculate its coordinates by solving the simultaneous equations $3x + y = 6$ and $x + 2y = 7$.

This situation is characteristic of the general case. As there are only two control variables, the feasible region can be illustrated well by a two-dimensional drawing. Suppose that the region formed by the constraints is bounded by straight lines, and is convex (that is, the corners all point outwards). Then, if the objective function to be maximised is of the form $ax + by$, where a and b are constants, its value is maximised at one of the vertices of the region.

In the special case when one of the edges of the region is parallel to the direction of the objective function line, the objective function may be maximised at two of the vertices, and at every point joining those two vertices. Exercise 8A Question 5 gives an example of this.

Exercise 8A

1   In each part, sketch the regions determined by the inequalities. Find the maximum value of x and the maximum value of y in each of the regions. Keep your sketches for Question 2.

(a) $x + 3y \leqslant 6$, $x \leqslant 3$, $x \geqslant 0$, $y \geqslant 0$

(b) $x + y \leqslant 4$, $x - y \leqslant 0$, $x \geqslant 0$, $y \leqslant 3$

(c) $-x + y \geqslant -3$, $-x + y \leqslant 3$, $y \leqslant 4$, $x \geqslant 0$, $y \geqslant 0$

(d) $x - 4y \leqslant 4$, $x + y \leqslant 5$, $x \geqslant 0$, $y \geqslant 0$

2   Maximise the objective function $x + 2y$ for each set of constraints in Question 1.

3   Maximise the function $y - x$ subject to the constraints $2x - y \geqslant -3$, $x - 2y \leqslant 3$, $2x + y \leqslant 11$, $x \geqslant 0$ and $y \geqslant 0$.

4   Minimise the function $y - x$ subject to the constraints in Question 3.

5   Maximise $3x + y$ subject to the constraints $2y \geqslant 3x$, $y + 3x \leqslant 9$, $x \geqslant 0$ and $y \geqslant 0$.

8.3   Linear programming problems

Here is the summary of the problem in Section 8.1, about making two different kinds of paper.

Maximise $x + y$,

subject to $2x + y \leqslant 16$,   (scrap paper)
$2x + 3y \leqslant 24$,   (timber)
$x \geqslant 0$,
$y \geqslant 0$.

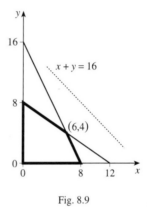

Fig. 8.9

The solution is shown in Fig. 8.9. The region which contains the allowable points has been highlighted, and the line $x + y = 16$ has been drawn with a dashed line. You can see that the point in the region which maximises $x + y$ is the point $(6, 4)$. The maximum value itself is therefore $6 + 4$, which is 10.

The maximum amount of paper which can be made per day is 10 tonnes.

In general, the region which contains the allowable points is called the **feasible region**. The variables x and y which describe the problem are called **control variables**. The constraints are called 'linear' constraints because they are closely related to straight lines.

Since World War II there have been major advances in the techniques for dealing with optimisation problems that have large numbers of linear constraints. In particular, computer software which can solve a wide range of practical problems is now readily available. In this chapter, you will learn a method for dealing with large-scale problems, but first you will gain experience with small-scale problems which can be solved graphically. This branch of mathematics is called **linear programming**, because of the connection with straight lines.

In general, for variables x, y, z, $\dots$, a combination of these variables is called **linear** if it is of the form

$ax + by + cz + \dots$, where a, b, c, $\dots$ are constants.

Example 8.3.1

Two machines, M_1 and M_2, are used to make two types of lamp, L_1 and L_2. Lamp L_1 requires the use of machine M_1 for 2 minutes and machine M_2 for 3 minutes. Lamp L_2 requires the use of machine M_1 for 4 minutes and machine M_2 for 3 minutes. The profit on lamp L_1 is £7 and the profit on lamp L_2 is £11. How can the profit per hour be maximised?

Define the control variables x and y to be the number of lamps L_1 and L_2 produced each hour. Then the profit per hour is £$(7x+11y)$, so $7x+11y$ needs to be maximised.

It is useful to lay out the information in tabular form.

Lamp	Time on M_1	Time on M_2
L_1	2 minutes	3 minutes
L_2	4 minutes	3 minutes
Time available	60 minutes	60 minutes

The constraints, apart from $x \geqslant 0$ and $y \geqslant 0$, are $2x+4y \leqslant 60$, arising from the use of M_1, and $3x+3y \leqslant 60$, arising from the use of M_2.

Summarising, and dividing the constraint inequalities by 2 and 3 respectively, the problem becomes:

maximise $P = 7x+11y$,

subject to $x+2y \leqslant 30$,   (machine M_1)
$\qquad\qquad\quad x+y \leqslant 20$,   (machine M_2)
$\qquad\qquad\quad x \geqslant 0$,
$\qquad\qquad\quad y \geqslant 0$.

The solution is shown in Fig. 8.10. The region which contains the allowable points has been highlighted, and the line $7x+11y = 231$ has been drawn to show the direction of $7x+11y = k$. You can see that the point in the region which maximises $7x+11y$ is the one marked in the diagram. By solving the equations $x+2y = 30$ and $x+y = 20$ simultaneously, you find that the point is $(10,10)$. The maximum value itself is therefore $7 \times 10 + 11 \times 10$, which is 180.

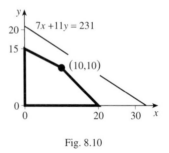

Fig. 8.10

The profit is maximised by making 10 of each lamp each hour.

An alternative method is to draw the graph to find all the vertices of the feasible region. Since you know that the objective function is maximised or minimised by the coordinates of a vertex, you can simply test each vertex in turn to find the best one. This method is used in the next example.

Example 8.3.2
A joiner makes two kinds of bookcase, standard and de luxe. The standard bookcase requires 4 square metres to make and store it, and the de luxe model requires 5 square metres, and there are only 61 square metres of space available. The standard model takes 30 minutes to make, and the de luxe model takes 40 minutes, and there are 480 minutes available in the day. The profit on a standard model is £50, and on a de luxe model it is £70. How should the joiner's time be spent?

The problem may be summarised as follows.

Maximise $\quad 50x + 70y,$

subject to $\quad 4x + 5y \leqslant 61, \quad$ (available space)
$\qquad\qquad\quad 30x + 40y \leqslant 480, \quad$ (available time)
$\qquad\qquad\quad x \geqslant 0,\ y \geqslant 0.$

From a graph, the coordinates of the feasible region are found to be $(0,0)$, $\left(15\frac{1}{4},0\right)$, $(4,9)$ and $(0,12)$.

The values of the objective function at these vertices in turn are 0, $762\frac{1}{2}$, 830 and 840. Since the largest value, 840, corresponds to the point $(0,12)$, the joiner should make only de luxe bookcases.

Note that the point $\left(15\frac{1}{4},0\right)$ does not give a practical solution. This is covered in Section 8.5.

8.4 Blending problems

Blending is an important and highly mathematical commercial activity, whether it be blending fruit juices, paint or margarine oils. Formulating constraints mathematically for blending problems can be quite complicated. The solution to Example 8.4.1 provides a useful illustration of the standard techniques.

Example 8.4.1

A blending company buys two types of fruit juice, A and B, from other suppliers. The details are summarised in the table below.

Juice	Orange juice	Lemon juice	Other	Cost per litre	Minimum weekly order
A	50%	0%	50%	40p	25 000 litres
B	20%	10%	70%	30p	30 000 litres

These juices are blended to produce a fruit juice which must contain at least 30% orange juice and at least 5% lemon juice. How can the company minimise the cost of producing at least 60 000 litres of juice per week?

Suppose the company uses x litres of A and y litres of B.

Since the new fruit juice has to contain 30% orange juice,

$$\frac{0.5x + 0.2y}{x + y} \geqslant 0.3,$$

which simplifies to give $2x \geqslant y$.

Similarly, the constraint on lemon juice gives

$$\frac{0.1y}{x + y} \geqslant 0.05,$$

which can be rearranged to give $y \geqslant x$.

The other constraints are the total requirement, which is $x + y \geqslant 60\,000$, and the minimum orders, which are $x \geqslant 25\,000$ and $y \geqslant 30\,000$.

Here is the summary of the problem.

Minimise $P = 0.4x + 0.3y$,

subject to $2x \geqslant y$,
$y \geqslant x$,
$x + y \geqslant 60\,000$,
$x \geqslant 25\,000$,
$y \geqslant 30\,000$.

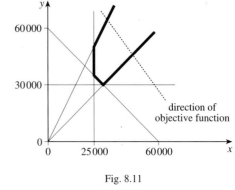

Fig. 8.11

From Fig. 8.11, the minimum occurs when $x = 25\,000$ and $y = 35\,000$, giving a cost of £20,500.

The next section deals with a complication which can arise in some linear programming problems.

8.5 Integer solutions

Consider the recycling plant example used in Section 8.1, and suppose that the availability of scrap paper and timber dropped to 13 and 21 tonnes per day respectively. The information is laid out in Table 8.12.

Raw material	Raw material per tonne of paper		Availability per day
	P_1	P_2	
Scrap paper	2 tonnes	1 tonne	13 tonnes
Timber	2 tonnes	3 tonnes	21 tonnes

Table 8.12

As a linear programming problem, this would be

maximise $x + y$,

subject to $2x + y \leqslant 13$,
$2x + 3y \leqslant 21$,
$x \geqslant 0, y \geqslant 0$.

If you work through the problem you will find that the maximum value of $x + y$ is 8.5, obtained when 4.5 tonnes of P_1 and 4 tonnes of P_2 are produced. In some contexts this output of 8.5 tonnes would be the required solution. However, there are circumstances where only integer solutions are appropriate. In this case, for example, the various contracts for the recycling plant's paper might be for whole numbers of tonnes. In that case, the linear programming problem is best formulated as follows.

Maximise $x + y$,

subject to $2x + y \leqslant 13$,
                $2x + 3y \leqslant 21$,
                $x \geqslant 0$, $y \geqslant 0$,
                x, y are integers.

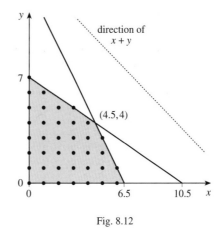

The integer points inside the feasible region are shown in Fig 8.12. The solution is 8 tonnes, obtained at three different points $(3,5)$, $(4,4)$ and $(5,3)$. Note that two of these are on the boundary of the feasible region, but not at a vertex, and $(4,4)$ is not even on the boundary.

Fig. 8.12

In some cases, the integer solution may be some distance from the vertex at which the 'normal' solution occurs. See Exercise 8B Question 5.

Exercise 8B

1   A company has 2400 assembly hours available for a trial run of two new models of calculator. The availability of components means that at most 400 of each can be manufactured initially. The assembly times and profits for the two models are as shown in the table. The total profit has to be maximised.

Model	Assembly hours	Profit
A	3	£7
B	4	£8

(a) Formulate this as a problem with integer solutions.

(b) Use a graphical method to maximise the total profit.

2   A small factory makes two types of valve, V and W, for profits of £5 and £3 respectively. Let x be the number of V and y be the number of W produced per day. Maximise the total daily profit subject to the constraints

   $x + 2y \leqslant 90$,   (machine hours)
   $2x + y \leqslant 60$.   (labour)

3   Due to market changes, the profit on each valve W of Question 2 changes to £p. For what values of p should the factory

(a) make only valve V,   (b) make only valve W?

4   A factory produces two items. Each day there are 160 labour hours available and 200 machine hours. Item 1 requires 2 hours of labour and 5 hours of machine time. Item 2 requires 4 hours of labour and 2 hours of machine time.

(a) Formulate the problem of maximising the total daily output of items as a linear programming problem.

(b) How should the production be divided between the two items?

(c) Suppose the profit is £50 on item 1 and £10 on item 2. How would this affect your answer to part (b)?

5 Solve these two linear programming problems.

(a) Maximise $2x + 3y,$

subject to $20x + 32y \leqslant 160,$
$3x - 2y \leqslant 0,$
$x \geqslant 0, y \geqslant 0.$

(b) Maximise $2x + 3y,$

subject to $20x + 32y \leqslant 160,$
$3x - 2y \leqslant 0,$
$x \geqslant 0, y \geqslant 0,$
x, y are integers.

6 A brand of margarine is made from two kinds of oil, which are refined and then blended.

Oil	Cost per kg	Hardness	Maximum daily production
X	£1.50	3.2	5000 kg
Y	£1.80	9.5	3000 kg

The margarine sells at £3.50 per kg and its hardness must be between 6 and 7.

(a) Formulate this as a linear programming problem to maximise the daily profit.

(b) How can the manufacturers maximise their daily profit?

7 Expected annual returns are 4% from savings accounts and 10% from shares. An investor requires an annual return of at least 7.5% and has up to £10,000 to invest. The investor is 'risk averse' and so wants to invest as much as possible in a savings account.

(a) Formulate this as a linear programming problem.

(b) Hence advise the investor.

8 The budget for a promotion run by a small company is £10,000. Full-page advertisements in regional newspapers cost £1200 each and have an estimated audience of 40 000 people. Advertisements on radio programmes cost £500 each and have an estimated audience of 18 000 people. It has been decided that at most ten of the advertisements will be on the radio. Assuming no overlaps between the various audiences, how many advertisements should be scheduled in each medium to maximise audience contact? What is the total cost and the total audience?

9 A company produces margarines by blending three oils, A, B and C. Here are the details for the next production run.

Oil	Cost per kg (£)	Availability (kg)
A	1.25	5000
B	1.60	10 000
C	1.82	10 000

Two brands of margarine are made, Regular and De luxe, selling at £2.50 per kilogram and £3.50 per kilogram respectively. Regular must consist of at most 30% oil A and at least 40% oil B. De luxe must consist of at most 40% oil B and at least 30% oil C. Formulate, but do not solve, the problem of maximising the profit by letting x, y and z be the number of kilograms of A, B and C, respectively, used for Regular and by letting u, v and w be the number of kilograms of A, B and C, respectively, used for De luxe.

Miscellaneous exercise 8

1 Gin is 45% alcohol by volume and tonic is non-alcoholic. It is required to mix gin-and-tonics which are at least 10% alcohol by volume and contain at least 200 ml of liquid but at most 30 ml of alcohol.

  (a) What are the least and greatest amounts of gin which such a drink could contain?

  (b) What are the least and the greatest amounts of tonic which such a drink could contain?

2 Solve the two linear programming problems:

  (a) Maximise $2x + 3y$,
       subject to $5x + 7y \leqslant 35$,
       $4x + 9y \leqslant 36$,
       $x \geqslant 0, y \geqslant 0$.

  (b) Maximise $2x + 3y$,
       subject to $5x + 7y \leqslant 35$,
       $4x + 9y \leqslant 36$,
       $x \geqslant 0, y \geqslant 0$,
       x, y are integers.

3 The following figures can be used to compare the three main forms of investment.

	Deposits	Gilts	Equities
Expected return[1]	1.5%	2.5%	8%
Risk factor[2]	0	20	60

  [1] Real return is inflation adjusted. Based upon the average return over the last 80 years. (Source: Barclays Capital Equity Gilt Study 1999)

  [2] Based upon the expected volatility of the invested capital.

  A retired person has £70,000 to invest to supplement their pension. A stockbroker recommends that they should have a mix of investments to give an expected return of at least 5.5% and an overall risk factor of at most 40. Subject to these constraints, the pensioner wishes to maximise the amount of money in fixed interest investment (gilts).

  (a) Let £x, £y and £z be the amounts invested in deposits, gilts and equities respectively. Show that the problem can be formulated as follows.

       Maximise y,
       subject to $x + y + z = 70\,000$, $8x + 6y \leqslant 5z$,
       $2x + y \geqslant z$, $x \geqslant 0, y \geqslant 0, z \geqslant 0$.

  (b) What main assumption has been made in this formulation of an investment problem?

  (c) Solve the linear programming problem of part (a). (Hint: substitute for z.)

4 (a) Sketch the feasible region for the following constraints.

       $-7x + 10y \leqslant 70$ $x + y \leqslant 15$ $x \leqslant 7$
       $7x - 4y \leqslant 28$ $21x + 7y \geqslant 63$ $5x + 11y \geqslant 55$
       $x, y \geqslant 0$.

  (b) What value of x maximises
       (i) $4x + 5y$,   (ii) $5x + 4y$?

5 A university has enough places for 5000 students. Government restrictions mean that at least 80% of the places must be given to UK students, but the remainder may be given to overseas students.

There are 2000 residential places available in the halls. All overseas students and at least one-third of the UK students must be given places in the halls.

The university gets £4000 in tuition fees for each UK student and £6000 for each overseas student. It wants to maximise the fees received.

Let x be the number of places given to UK students and y be the number of places given to overseas students.

(a) Explain, briefly, why the problem requires the function $P = 4000x + 6000y$ to be maximised.

(b) The constraints of the problem are

$$x + y \leqslant 5000,$$
$$4y \leqslant x,$$
$$\tfrac{1}{3}x + y \leqslant 2000,$$
$$x \geqslant 0 \text{ and } y \geqslant 0.$$

Explain why

(i) $4y \leqslant x$, and   (ii) $\tfrac{1}{3}x + y \leqslant 2000$.

The feasible region for the problem is shown in the figure.

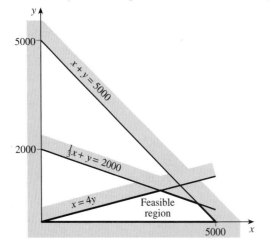

(c) Write down the vertices of the feasible region which lie on the x-axis. Use simultaneous equations to calculate the coordinates of the other vertices of the feasible region (to the nearest whole number), and hence calculate the value of P at each vertex.

(d) Use your answer to (c) to advise the university on how many places they should give to UK students, and how many to overseas students, to maximise the fees received.

(OCR)

6 A company manufactures two kinds of robot, the Brainy and the Superbrainy. After production, each robot is tested for its coordination and its logic. The company wants to maximise its profit from the sale of the robots. You may assume that every robot manufactured is sold. The table below shows the times required by these tests, the time available each week, and the profit per robot.

	Coordination test (hours)	Logic test (hours)	Profit per robot (£)
Brainy	6	3	2400
Superbrainy	3	4	3000
Time available (hours)	60	60	

This problem is being modelled using a linear programming formulation:

x = number of Brainy robots manufactured per week;

y = number of Superbrainy robots manufactured per week.

Maximise $P = 2400x + 3000y$.

(a) Write down the four constraints for this problem.

(b) Represent the constraints graphically, marking the feasible region clearly.

(c) Showing your method clearly, solve the linear programming problem.   (OCR)

7 Lou Zitt has a budget of £2000 to spend on storage units for his office. The storage units must not cover more than 50 m^2 of floor space. Lou wants to maximise the storage capacity.

The three types of storage unit that he can choose from are shown below.

Type	Storage capacity (m^3)	Floor space covered (m^2)	Cost (£)
Antique pine units	2	1	100
Beech wood units	9	4	500
Cedar wood units	5	3	200

Suppose that Lou buys a antique pine units, b beech wood units and c cedar wood units.

(a) Write down two constraints that must be satisfied by a, b and c, other than $a \geqslant 0$, $b \geqslant 0$ and $c \geqslant 0$.

(b) Write down the objective function for this problem.

(c) Set up the problem as an LP formulation. ('LP' stands for 'linear programming'.) You are not expected to solve the problem.

(d) Identify which aspect of the original problem has been overlooked in the LP formulation.

Because of the shape of the office, Lou also needs to consider the widths of the units. The antique pine units are 1 metre wide, the beech wood units are 2 metres wide and the cedar wood units are 3 metres wide. The total width of the units cannot exceed 20 metres.

(e) Show how to incorporate this additional restriction into your LP formulation.   (OCR)

8 A factory manufactures three items; screws, nuts and bolts.

The items are first produced on a machine which is available for 4 hours per day. The machine takes 6 minutes to produce a screw, 4 minutes to produce a nut and 2 minutes to produce a bolt. The items are then cleaned on a machine that is available for 55 minutes per day. Each screw takes 30 seconds to clean, each nut takes 40 seconds to clean and each bolt takes 60 seconds to clean.

(a) An apprentice at the factory produces x screws, y nuts and z bolts in a day. Find and simplify two inequalities each involving x, y and z, that model the conditions given above.

(b) As a further requirement the apprentice must produce the same number of bolts as nuts each day.

(i) Show that, with this additional constraint, the two inequalities found in part (a) become $x + y \leqslant 40$ and $3x + 10y \leqslant 330$.

(ii) Draw a suitable diagram to represent this problem graphically, indicating the feasible region.

(iii) The apprentice has to make the largest possible total number of items each day. Draw an objective line that will represent his total daily output, T. Hence indicate the vertex that will correspond to the maximum value of T.

(iv) Calculate the maximum value of T.

(v) On a particular day the cleaning machine is available for only 48 minutes. Find the maximum number of items that the apprentice can make during this particular day.

(AQA)

9 A company makes two types of door, standard and luxury. Both types of door require the use of two different machines A and B.

Both types of door require 90 minutes on machine A. A standard door requires 60 minutes on machine B but a luxury door requires 120 minutes on this machine. During any one week machine A can be used for a maximum of 20 hours and machine B can be used for a maximum of 25 hours.

The company makes a profit of £10 on each standard door and £12 on each luxury door. In a week the company makes x standard doors and y luxury doors.

(a) Show that the above information can be modelled by the following inequalities.

$$x \geqslant 0, \quad y \geqslant 0, \quad 3x + 3y \leqslant 40, \quad x + 2y \leqslant 25$$

(b) (i) Draw a suitable diagram to represent the problem graphically, indicating the feasible region.

(ii) Draw an objective line that will represent the company's profit for the week, £P. Hence indicate the vertex, V, that could correspond to the maximum value of P.

(iii) State why this maximum value of P cannot be achieved.

(iv) Find values of x and y that will maximise the company's profit and calculate this profit.

(AQA)

10 An insurance saleswoman can sell two types of policy, pension policies and life assurance policies.

Head-office require her to sell at least three policies of each type per week.

Regulations stipulate that a pension policy needs 60 minutes of explanation but a life assurance policy needs 20 minutes of explanation.

The saleswoman knows that she can sell policies only in an evening and that in a normal week she has 15 hours available to sell policies.

Each pension policy has an annual premium income (API) of £600 whereas each life assurance policy has an API of £120.

Head-office requires a salesperson to sell, in a week, policies with a total API of at least £4800.

The saleswoman is paid a commission on each policy she sells. For each pension policy she is paid £48 and for each life assurance policy she is paid £36.

In a week the saleswoman sells x pension policies and y life assurance policies.

(a) (i) Show that $3x + y \leqslant 45$.

(ii) Find three further inequalities in x and y that model the saleswoman's situation.

(b) (i) Draw a suitable diagram to represent this problem graphically, indicating the feasible region.

(ii) Draw the line that will represent a weekly commission of £576. Hence find the vertex that will maximise her weekly commission.

(c) (i) State the values of x and y that maximise her commission.

(ii) If the saleswoman is paid this commission each week throughout a 45 week working year, calculate her income for the year.

(d) During a promotional week, head-office changes her commission structure so that a pension policy pays £90 and a life assurance policy pays £18. All other constraints remain the same.

(i) She was paid £1170 in commission for the week. Determine one possible pair of values of x and y.

(ii) Calculate her maximum possible commission for the week. (AQA)

Revision exercise

1 Consider the following algorithm which operates on two positive integers, X and Y.

READ X, Y
LABEL A
   IF $X > Y$ THEN $X = X - Y$
   IF $Y > X$ THEN $Y = Y - X$
   IF $X \neq Y$ THEN GOTO A
PRINT X

(a) Trace the algorithm in the case when $X = 24$ and $Y = 20$.

(b) Write down the purpose of this algorithm.   (AQA)

2 The following matrix represents the distances between vertices in an undirected network. A missing entry indicates that there is no direct connection.

		From				
		A	B	C	D	E
	A	–	2	1	6	3
	B	2	–	5	–	10
To	C	1	5	–	2	–
	D	6	–	2	–	6
	E	3	10	–	6	–

(a) Draw the network.

(b) Use an appropriate algorithm to find the graph which is a minimum connector for the vertices of the network. Start from A and list the order in which you include edges. Give the length of your connector.

(c) A Hamiltonian cycle is a path visiting each vertex once and only once, and returning to the initial vertex. List all Hamiltonian cycles, taking vertex A as the initial and final vertex, and find a Hamiltonian cycle with the shortest length.

(d) It is often said that twice the length of the minimum connector is an upper bound for the solution to the travelling salesperson problem. Explain why, in this network, the minimum Hamiltonian cycle is greater than twice the length of the minimum connector.   (AQA)

3 A company producing dining chairs and tables requires a production plan for the next month. The company has £10,000 budgeted to buy materials. Chairs each require £20 of materials and tables £100. Tables each need 15 hours of work from craftsmen and chairs each need 4 hours. There are 1950 hours of craftsman time available per month. The company sells chairs at £80 each and tables at £350. A production plan is required which maximises potential income.

(a) Formulate the problem as a linear programming problem.

(b) Use a graphical method to solve the problem.   (AQA, adapted)

4 A mathematician is writing a chapter of a book. In this chapter she wishes to start from result A, which was proved in an earlier chapter, to prove results B, C, D and E. There are many ways in which she can do this, since she can prove some results from others. She would like to do it as efficiently as possible, so that the total number of lines of proof is as small as possible.

The numbers of lines of proof required to establish one result directly from another are given in the following table:

		Result to be proved			
		B	C	D	E
	A	10	9	–	15
	B	–	15	20	7
Proved result	C	15	–	11	12
	D	20	11	–	5
	E	7	12	5	–

For example, she can prove B from A in 10 lines.

(a) Of the two graphs shown, one represents a possible solution, the other does not. State with a reason which does not represent a solution, and give the number of lines of proof required for the other.

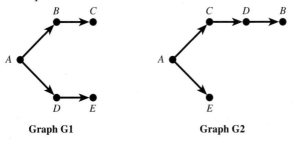

Graph G1   **Graph G2**

(b) Use the following algorithm to find an efficient way for the mathematician to prove all the results B, C, D and E from A. Draw the graph representing your solution and give the total number of lines of proof.

Step 1 Start with A proved.

Step 2 Prove the next result which can be proved in the minimum number of lines from a proved result.

Step 3 Repeat Step 2 until all results are proved.

(c) Suppose that the mathematician subsequently discovers that she can prove C from D in only 8 instead of 11 lines. (It still takes 11 lines to prove D from C, and all other figures are similarly unaffected.)

Draw a graph representing an improved solution.

Explain why the algorithm does not succeed in finding an improved solution. (AQA)

5 The following network shows two islands each with seven small towns. One road bridge connects the two islands. Values shown represent distances by road, in miles.

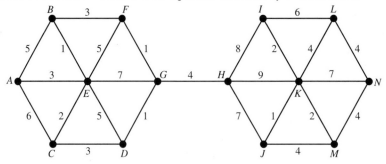

(a) Use Dijkstra's algorithm to find the shortest distance between A and N, stating the route.

A new road bridge is to be constructed connecting the two islands. A feasibility study produces two possible bridge routes. The first option, connecting F and I, would be of length 11 miles. The second option, connecting D and J, would be of length 10 miles.

(b) For each of these options, determine how many of the distances by road between A and the other 13 towns would be shortened.

6 The graph is a representation of a system of roads. The lengths of the roads are shown in metres.

(a) List the odd vertices in the graph.

(b) Explain why the graph is not Eulerian.

(c) By considering ways of pairing the odd vertices, find the shortest route, starting and finishing at A, and traversing each road at least once.

State the length of your route.   (AQA)

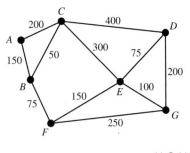

7 The distances, in miles, between six towns are given by the following matrix.

	A	B	C	D	E	F
A	–	3	5	10	13	19
B	3	–	4	7	13	23
C	5	4	–	7	10	22
D	10	7	7	–	17	18
E	13	13	10	17	–	9
F	19	23	22	18	9	–

(a) Using Prim's algorithm and showing your working at each stage, find a minimum spanning tree for these six towns.

(b) State the length of your minimum spanning tree.

(c) When information is provided in matrix form, explain why Prim's algorithm, in preference to Kruskal's algorithm, is normally used to find a minimum spanning tree.

(AQA)

8 A Council has five committees: Cleansing (*C*), Finance (*F*), General Purposes (*G*), Parks (*P*) and Roads (*R*). The following pairs of committees have members in common:

General Purposes and Cleansing
General Purposes and Finance
General Purposes and Parks
General Purposes and Roads
Parks and Roads
Roads and Finance
Finance and Cleansing.

(a) Represent this information on a graph. Your graph should have five vertices, one for each committee. The edges should indicate where committees have a member in common.

Each committee must meet once a week, either on Monday, Tuesday or Wednesday. Committees with members in common must not be scheduled at the same time.

(b) Apply the following algorithm for scheduling the meetings. Show clearly the result of each step.

  1 Schedule Cleansing for Monday.

  2 Choose the next committee in alphabetical order and schedule it for the first day possible from Monday, Tuesday or Wednesday, ensuring that it is not scheduled at the same time as a scheduled committee with which it shares a member.

  3 If this is not possible then stop.

  4 If all committees are now scheduled then stop, otherwise return to step 2.

(c) Find a feasible weekly schedule.   (AQA)

9 Use a shortest path algorithm to find a path of least weight from *A* to *C* in the following weighted network.

You are required to show sufficient working to demonstrate your application of the algorithm — the answer alone will not be sufficient.

Give your least weight path and its total weight.   (AQA)

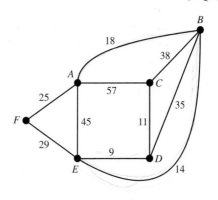

10 The Chinese Postman (Route Inspection) Problem is to find the shortest route which traverses every edge in a network at least once. An algorithm for this involves pairing the vertices of odd degree in the network. Thus, if a network has 4 odd vertices, *A*, *B*, *C* and *D*, then one pairing is *A* with *B* and *C* with *D*.

(a) How many ways are there of pairing 4 odd vertices?

(b) How many ways are there of pairing 6 odd vertices?

(c) How many ways are there of pairing 20 odd vertices?   (AQA)

11 The travelling salesperson problem is to find the shortest Hamiltonian cycle in a network, that is, the shortest path visiting each vertex once and only once and returning to the initial vertex.

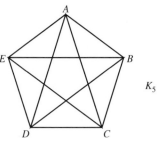

   (a) Regarding $ABCDEA$ as different from $AEDCBA$, how many different Hamiltonian cycles are there in the graph K_5?

   (b) How many Hamiltonian cycles are there in K_{50}?

A fast computer takes 1 second to find the lengths of 10 million such cycles. Approximately how many years will it take to find the lengths of all of them?   **(AQA)**

12 A building company has acquired a building site on which to build residential dwellings. It has permission to build at least 12 but not more than 16 dwellings. The company can build a combination of houses and bungalows on the site but it must build at least 4 of each.

   Each house needs a plot of size 450 m^2 and will have a floor area of 200 m^2.

   Each bungalow needs a plot of size 600 m^2 and will have a floor area of 150 m^2.

   The cost of a plot is £50 per m^2 and the building costs are £100 per m^2 of floor area.

   The total value of land which can be used for building plots must not exceed £450,000.

   The total building costs must not exceed £300,000.

The company builds x houses and y bungalows.

   (a) Show that the company's situation can be modelled by the following inequalities.

$$12 \leqslant x + y \leqslant 16$$
$$x \geqslant 4$$
$$y \geqslant 4$$
$$3x + 4y \leqslant 60$$
$$4x + 3y \leqslant 60$$

   (b) Draw a suitable diagram to represent this problem graphically, indicating the feasible region.

   (c) The company sells all the houses and bungalows at a profit of £10,000 per dwelling. Find the minimum profit that the company is sure to make on this building site.

      List all the different pairs of values of x and y that would produce this minimum profit.

   (d) An alternative pricing structure is proposed in which houses and bungalows are all sold at the same price of £S. The company maximises the profit and this total profit is £190,000.

      Find the largest and smallest possible values of S.

13 The following matrix shows the costs of connecting together each possible pair from six computer terminals:

$$
\begin{array}{c c c c c c c}
 & A & B & C & D & E & F \\
A & - & 120 & 200 & 140 & 135 & 250 \\
B & 120 & - & 230 & 75 & 130 & 80 \\
C & 200 & 230 & - & 160 & 160 & 120 \\
D & 140 & 75 & 160 & - & 200 & 85 \\
E & 135 & 130 & 160 & 200 & - & 150 \\
F & 250 & 80 & 120 & 85 & 150 & -
\end{array}
$$

The computers are to be connected together so that, for any pair of computers, there should be either a direct link between them or a link via one or more other computers. Use an appropriate algorithm to find the cheapest way of connecting these computers. Show your result on a network and give the total cost.

Ensure that you show clearly the steps of the algorithm. Stating the correct answer without showing how you achieved it is not sufficient. (AQA)

14 A woman invests £200 on January 1 for each of three years in a fixed income bond that pays interest of 8 per cent per annum, the interest being added to her account at the end of each year.

The following algorithm gives the total value of her investment after the three-year period.

$A = 0$
FOR $I = 1$ TO 3
$A = A + 200$
$A = 1.08 \times A$
NEXT I
PRINT A

(a) Trace the algorithm.

(b) Explain how the algorithm could be amended to give her the value of her investment at the end of each year, after interest for that year has been added.

(c) Write a modified algorithm that would find the value, after a period of N years, of an investment of £P, invested at the start of each year, in a bond paying a constant rate of interest of R per cent per annum. (AQA)

Mock examination 1

Time 1 hour 20 minutes

Answer all the questions.

1 The following matrix shows the distances, in miles, between six towns.

	A	B	C	D	E	F
A	–	14	21	12	16	20
B	14	–	25	6	11	9
C	21	25	–	16	17	14
D	12	6	16	–	21	10
E	16	11	17	21	–	16
F	20	9	14	10	16	–

(a) Using Kruskal's algorithm and showing your working at each stage, find the minimum spanning tree for these six towns. [4]

(b) State the length of your minimum spanning tree. [1]

[5]

2 Four members of a horticultural society have decided to each prepare examples of one type of flower for a show. Sandy prefers growing irises, but also grows primulas and roses, Clay specialises in primulas, Chalky grows irises and primulas and Pete prefers growing roses, but is also good at growing azaleas.

(a) Show this information on a bipartite graph. [2]

(b) On your diagram, show the matching based upon Clay, Pete and Sandy growing their favourite flowers. Demonstrate, by using an algorithm to find an alternating path from this initial matching, how a selection could be made so that all four flowers are prepared for the show. [5]

[7]

3 The time, in minutes, for each section of a journey is shown in the diagram.

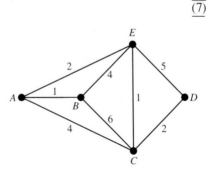

(a) Use Dijkstra's algorithm to find the minimum time for the journey *AD* and state the route which should be used. [5]

(b) The section *AC* is improved so that the journey time *AD* is reduced. Given that the journey time from *A* to *E* is *not* reduced by this improved link, find upper and lower bounds for *x*, the time in minutes, for the new section *AC*. [4]

[9]

4 Use the Shell Sort algorithm to arrange the following words into alphabetical order, showing the new arrangement at each stage.

     Coati, Foumart, Avadavat, Dhole, Blesmol, Hinny, Eland, Grison.

Count the number of comparisons required at each stage.   [9]

(9)

5 The network shows the times, in minutes, to cycle between four villages. It is required to find a Hamiltonian cycle of minimal time.

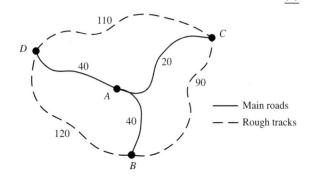

(a) Apply a greedy algorithm from B to obtain an upper bound to the problem.   [3]

(b) By initially ignoring town D, find a lower bound. [3]

(c) List all the Hamiltonian cycles for this network and hence find the actual minimal time for a Hamiltonian cycle.   [3]

(d) In practice, what would be the shortest time needed for a journey starting and finishing at A and visiting B, C and D? Why is this answer smaller than the lower bound of part (b)?   [4]

(13)

6 A large manufacturing company is intending to reduce the size of its work force by at least 200, in order to cut its annual wage bill by at least £3 million. At present, the company employs 300 Machine Operatives, each paid £14,000 per annum, and 250 Senior Machine Operatives, each paid £18,000 per annum. An analyst reckons that the loss of each Machine Operative will reduce annual output by £24,000 and that the loss of each Senior Machine Operative will reduce annual output by £30,000. Let x and y be the number of redundancies of Machine Operatives and Senior Machine Operatives, respectively.

(a) Write down a linear programme to find the optimal mix of redundancies to reduce output by as little as possible.   [5]

(b) Draw a suitable diagram to represent this problem graphically, indicating the feasible region.   [4]

(c) Draw an objective line to represent the reduction in output, R. Hence indicate the vertex that will correspond to the minimum value of R and calculate this value.   [4]

(d) The company accountant believes that the analyst has underestimated the loss of output resulting from the loss of a Senior Machine Operative. By how much would this loss need to be increased to alter the optimal mix of redundancies?   [4]

(17)

Mock examination 2

Time 1 hour 20 minutes

Answer all the questions.

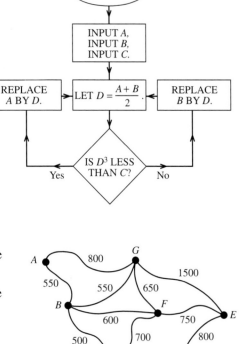

1 Consider the flow diagram.

(a) For inputs of $A = 2$, $B = 3$ and $C = 10$, perform the first four passes through the

LET $D = \dfrac{A + B}{2}$ box.　　　　[4]

(b) What is this procedure designed to do?　　　　[2]

(c) State two problems with the procedure defined by this flow diagram.　　　　[2]

$\overline{(8)}$

2 A warden has to patrol the paths shown in the diagram, where all distances are in metres.

(a) Find an optimal 'Chinese Postman' route that starts and finishes at A. State the length of this route.　　　　[3]

The warden decides to clear an overgrown path which joins two of the places already on the diagram.

(b) She will then be able to walk along every path without repeating any path. Write down the two places which this path links, explaining your answer.　　　　[2]

(c) Given that the addition of this new path would not affect the distance she must walk on her patrol, find the length of the overgrown path.　　　　[2]

$\overline{(7)}$

3 A linear programming problem is:

maximise　　　$P = 3x + 4y$

subject to　　　$x + y \leqslant 8$,
　　　　　　　　$x + 3y \leqslant 15$,
　　　　　　　　$x \geqslant 0$, $y \geqslant 1$.

(a) Draw a suitable diagram to enable the problem to be solved graphically, indicating the feasible region and the direction of the objective line.　　　　[6]

(b) Use your diagram to find the maximum value of P.　　　　[3]

(c) The best integer solution to the problem gives $P = 27$. Find this solution.　　　　[2]

$\overline{(11)}$

4 Use the Shuttle Sort algorithm to rearrange the following numbers into ascending order. Show the result of each pass.

  9, 7, 5, 13, 2, 8, 6, 16   [6]

                                                                                         $\overline{(6)}$

5 (a) Explain what is meant by

  (i) K_n,   (ii) a Hamiltonian cycle.   [4]

 (b) Show that the number of different Hamiltonian cycles in K_n is $\frac{1}{2}(n-1)!$.   [2]

 (c) The graph shown is $K_{3,3}$. How many different Hamiltonian cycles are there in this graph?

  (Do not count a cycle taken in reverse order as different from the original.)   [2]

 (d) How many different Hamiltonian cycles are there in

  (i) $K_{4,4}$,   (ii) $K_{n,n}$?   [5]

                                                                                         $\overline{(13)}$

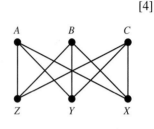

6 (a) Use Dijkstra's algorithm to find the shortest distance from A to G in the network.   [4]

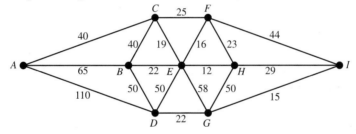

 (b) Describe how to use Dijkstra's algorithm to find the path corresponding to a shortest distance. Complete this procedure for the shortest distance of part (a).   [3]

 (c) Use Dijkstra's algorithm to show that the two possible expressions, in terms of x, for the minimum time to travel from R to U are

   4   and $2 + x$.   [3]

 (d) Find the three possible shortest distances from R to T. Hence find the ranges of possible values of x for which the shortest path from R to T is

  (i) $R S V U T$,   (ii) $R S U T$,   (iii) $R S T$.   [5]

                                                                                         $\overline{(15)}$

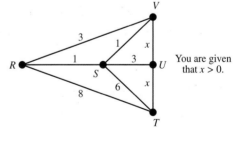

You are given that $x > 0$.

Answers

1 Algorithms

Exercise 1A (page 5)

1 (a) 10 comparisons, 10 swaps
   (b) 10 comparisons, 10 swaps
   (c) For lists in reverse order, both algorithms require the same number of comparisons and swaps.

2 (a) 15 (b) $\frac{1}{2}n(n-1)$

3 4 1 6 8 2, 1 4 6 8 2, 1 4 6 8 2, 1 4 6 8 2, 1 2 4 6 8
   7 comparisons, 4 swaps

4 (a) $n-1$ (b) 10 comparisons, 2 swaps plus any that you make in your own algorithm.

5 (a) 7, the sum of m and n.
     It will work only if m is a positive integer. The value of n does not matter.
   (b) 12, the product of m and n.
     It will work only if m is a positive integer. The value of n does not matter.

Exercise 1B (page 11)

1 (a) The process never terminates because N never becomes zero.
   (b) Step 7 could be changed to 'If $N>0$, then go to Step 3. Otherwise stop.'

2 3 1 2 6 5 9 8 7   4 comparisons
   2 1 3 6 5 7 8 9   7 comparisons
   1 2 3 5 6 7 8 9   8 comparisons
   19 comparisons

3 (a) Using the first element as the pivot: at each stage, and putting the pivot in bold type:
     Black, Green, Orange, **Pink**, Red, White
     Black, Green, Orange, **Pink**, **Red**, White
     Black, **Green**, Orange, **Pink**, **Red**, White
   (b) 15   (c) $\frac{1}{2}n(n-1)$

4 (a)
     5 7 2 8 6 **9** 11 7
     2 **5** 7 8 6 **9** 11 17
     2 **5** 6 **7** 8 **9** **11** 17

   (b) (i) 28   (ii) $\frac{1}{2}n(n-1)$

5 (a) (i)

47	69	8	52
47	69	8	52
8	47	69	52
8	47	52	69

     (ii) Shuttle Sort

  (b)

	4	10	3	7	2	1	8	11	7	12
$N=5$	1	8	3	7	2	4	10	11	7	12
$N=2$	1	4	2	7	3	8	7	11	10	12
$N=1$	1	2	3	4	7	7	8	10	11	12

Miscellaneous exercise 1 (page 14)

1 (a) (i) There are two roots.
     (ii) There is a repeated root.
     (iii) There are no roots.
   (b) It describes the roots of the equation $ax^2+bx+c=0$.

2 (a) 1.414 215 686, 1.732 050 81, 2.236 068 896
   (b) It finds $\sqrt{x}$.

3 (a) (i) 3   (ii) 2   (iii) 1
   (b) The greatest common factor of X and Y.

4

X	11	5	2	1	0
Y	9	18	36	72	72
T	0	9	27	27	99

   It multiplies X and Y.

5 (a) 8; 0
     8, 12; 1
     2, 8, 12; 1
     2, 8, 12, 54; 3
     2, 8, 12, 23, 54; 4
     2, 8, 12, 23, 31, 54; 5
   (b) 2, 8, 12, 23, 31, 54
   (c) $\frac{1}{2}n(n-1)$

6 (a)

	C	S	T	D
Start	0.8660	3.0000	3.4641	0.4641
1st	0.9659	3.1058	3.2154	0.1096
2nd	0.9914	3.1326	3.1597	0.0270
3rd	0.9979	3.1394	3.1461	0.0067

(b) 3

(c) Looks to be about 0.25.

(d) 0.4641×0.25^n

7 (a) (i) To initialise MIN

(ii) Next I

(iii) PRINT MIN

(b) 2   INPUT MARK

3   IF MARK < 0 THEN GO TO 7

Any set of marks is then input with a final negative marker.

(c) 1   SET MAX $= 0$

2   FOR $I = 1$ TO 50

3   INPUT MARK

4   IF MARK $>$ MAX

5   THEN MAX $=$ MARK

6   NEXT I

7   PRINT MAX

8 (a) (i) To initialise the variables

(ii) The J loop is performed for each value of I.

(iii) As a counter

(b) $I = 2, J = 3, X = 6$

9 (a) (i)

I	J	M	$X = S(M)$?	$X < S(M)$?
1	8	4	No	No
5		6	No	No
7		7	Yes	

7 is printed.

(ii)

I	J	M	$X = S(M)$?	$X < S(M)$?
1	8	4	No	No
5		6	No	No
7		7	No	No
8		8	No	Yes
8	7			

At this stage $I > J$, so FAIL is printed.

(b) 10, 5, 2, 1

10 (a) 3 4 1 5 2

(b) $n - 1$

(c) No random number generated is wasted in this algorithm, but many are wasted in the earlier algorithm.

2 Graphs and networks

Exercise 2A (page 24)

1 (a) Eulerian   (b) neither

(c) semi-Eulerian   (d) Eulerian

2 Consider the closed trail containing every edge precisely once. Each time a vertex occurs it has an edge going in and an edge coming out. (This applies even to the initial and the final vertices if you consider them together.) Each vertex is therefore at the end of an even number of edges, and therefore has even order.

3 (a)   (b)

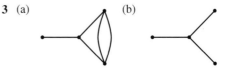

4 Yes. Start or finish in the top left room or the bottom left room.

5 Two towns linked by a motorway and by one or more local roads.

6 (a) $n - 1$ (b) For odd values of n.

7 (a) rs

(b) $K_{r,s}$ is Eulerian if and only if r and s are both even. It is semi-Eulerian either if $r = 1$ and $s = 1$, or if $r = 2$ and s is odd, or if $s = 2$ and r is odd.

8 (a) $A, B, C, D \to FS, HS, CE, ME$

(b) 2, Brian/David $\to$ Home Sec./Chancellor

Exercise 2B (page 29)

1 (a) Times from city A to city B, and from city B to city A could depend on road works or congestion, which may affect the two directions differently.

(b) (i) DC circuits   (ii) AC circuits

2 (a)

$$\begin{array}{c} & A & B & C & D & E & F \\ \begin{array}{c} A \\ B \\ C \\ D \\ E \\ F \end{array} & \begin{pmatrix} - & - & 1 & 6 & 7 & 8 \\ - & - & 2 & 3 & 4 & 3 \\ 1 & 2 & - & 7 & - & 2 \\ 6 & 3 & 7 & - & 5 & - \\ 7 & 4 & - & 5 & - & 9 \\ 8 & 3 & 2 & - & 9 & - \end{pmatrix} \end{array}$$

(b)
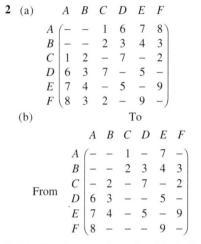

To

$$\begin{array}{c} & A & B & C & D & E & F \\ \text{From} & \begin{array}{c} A \\ B \\ C \\ D \\ E \\ F \end{array} & \begin{pmatrix} - & - & 1 & - & 7 & - \\ - & - & 2 & 3 & 4 & 3 \\ - & 2 & - & 7 & - & 2 \\ 6 & 3 & - & - & 5 & - \\ 7 & 4 & - & 5 & - & 9 \\ 8 & - & - & - & 9 & - \end{pmatrix} \end{array}$$

3 (a) Use the two edges of weight 2, the three edges of weight 3 and the edge *CF* of weight 4, giving a total of 17.

(b) The route is *ACDEG* making a total of 10.

4 $H = 2C + 2$

5
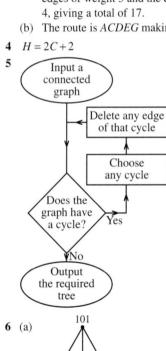

6 (a)
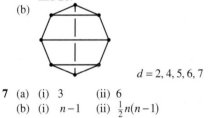

(b) It is possible to tell if a single error has occurred in the transmission.

7 (a) $\sum h_i = 2H$

(b) The sum of all the orders is $2H$.

Miscellaneous exercise 2 (page 30)

1 There is 1 tree with 3 vertices, 2 trees with 4 vertices, 3 trees with 5 vertices and 6 trees with 6 vertices.

2 (a) There are two odd vertices, the two islands on the right, so the trail must start on one of these islands and finish on the other.

(b) No

3 (a) *AB, ACB, ADB, ACDB, ADCB*

(b) $1 + 3 + 6 + 6 = 16$

(c) K_5; all its vertices have even order.

4 Draw cycle *ABCIE*. Join *BE* and *BI* inside the cycle. Join *AHFI* and *ADGC* outside the cycle.

5 (a) *ABCDEA* is a cycle. The chords crossing the circle are *AD*, *BD*, *BE* and *CE*. Call these *x*, *y*, *z* and *t*. There are now edges joining *x* to *z* and *t*, and *y* to *z* and *t*. This is a bipartite graph, with *x* and *y* in one set, and *z* and *t* in the other. Choosing *x* and *y*, that is, *AD* and *BD*, you can draw them outside the 'pentagon' to make a planar graph.

(b) Choose *ABCDEFA* as the cycle. The chords crossing the circle are *AD*, *BE* and *CF*. Call these *x*, *y* and *z*. The new graph is non-bipartite, so the original graph is not planar.

(c) There is no cycle which includes *C*, so stop. (However, the original graph is clearly planar.)

6 (a) The possible values of *d* are 2, 4 and 6, and the corresponding numbers of edges are 7, 14 and 21.

(b)
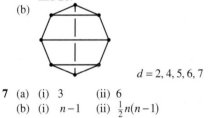

$d = 2, 4, 5, 6, 7$

7 (a) (i) 3   (ii) 6

(b) (i) $n - 1$ (ii) $\frac{1}{2}n(n-1)$

3 Minimum connector problems

Exercise 3A (page 37)

1 You should find 16 spanning trees.

2 (a) There are 14 spanning trees.

(b) The minimum spanning tree contains the edges with weights 27, 28, 31, 36, 43. The weight is 165.

(c) The order of choice is 43, 27, 31, 28, 36.

3 The cheapest way costs £1500, and consists of the edges *HL*, *ML*, *LC*, and *CI*.

5 The edges used are two of weight 3, one each of weights 5 and 6, two of weight 7 and one of weight 8. The total length is 39.

6 (a) When its removal would disconnect the graph.

   (b) Step 1 Find the edge of greatest weight whose removal does not disconnect the graph. Stop if no such edge exists.

   Step 2 Remove this edge from the graph and return to Step 1.

Exercise 3B (page 41)

1 (a) *AB*, *BH*, *BG*, *AC*, *CE*, *CD*, *AF* in that order. Total length 215 km.

   (b)
	A	B	C	D	E	F	G	H
A	–	20	27	50	60	30	24	50
B	20	–	50	60	50	65	30	30
C	27	50	–	30	10	80	80	75
D	50	60	30	–	33	70	85	100
E	60	50	10	33	–	85	75	55
F	30	65	80	70	85	–	70	100
G	24	30	80	85	75	70	–	45
H	50	30	75	100	55	100	45	–

   The minimum connector consists of the edges *AB*, *AG*, *AC*, *CE*, *BH*, *AF*, *CD* and takes 171 minutes.

   (c) The two minimum connectors are different. The route of least length connecting *G* to other points is 30 km from *G* to *B* which takes 30 minutes. The connection of shortest time is the motorway route of 40 km from *G* to *A* which takes 24 minutes.

2 (a) Starting from A, the minimum spanning tree consists of the following edges, added in this order: *AB*, *BD*, *DE*, *DC*, *EF*. The total cost is £240.

   (b) This has no effect because the total cost of each spanning tree is increased by the same proportion.

   (c) It is now better to connect *C* to *A*, rather than to *D*. The total cost is £300.

3 (a) The minimum connector is, in order: Paris – Orléans – Tours – Le Mans – Poitiers – Dijon – St-Etienne – Grenoble – Marseilles – Nice. The length is 1574 km.

   (b) The length is increased by only 99 km. Geneva is linked to Grenoble and Dijon, and the Dijon – St-Etienne link is dropped.

Miscellaneous exercise 3 (page 47)

1 New York – Washington – Chicago – Dallas – Denver – Los Angeles; 3150 miles

2 (a) The edges are: *BF*, *BD*, *BA*, *AC*, *CG*, *CE*. The length is 1420 metres.

   (b) *AC* is replaced by *DC*, and the length is increased by 100 metres.

3 In order, *BF*, *BD* and *AC* in either order, *AB*, *CG*, *CE*.

4 (a) *G* would need 10 edges.

   (b) (i) $7 + 7 + 7 + 9 = 30$

   (ii) The 4 shortest edges might form cycle(s).

   (iii)

   7   7   9   11

   The position of the other four edges is arbitrary.

5 For a connected graph with *n* vertices,

   Step 1 Choose the edge of greatest weight.

   Step 2 Choose from those edges remaining the edge of greatest weight which does not form a cycle with already chosen edges.

   Step 3 Repeat Step 2 until *n* − 1 edges have been chosen.

   Lo – Br, Lo – Bi, N – Li, Bi – Li, Lo – Le, Lo – S, Li – Ld, N – M, N – Sh. Total 1273 km.

6 (a) 42 cm   (b) By 7 cm to 35 cm

7 (a) The order is *AD*, *AE*, *EF*, *FB*, *FC*, with a total cost of £69 .

   (b) The furthest towns on the minimum connector are *D* and *C*. The route is *DAEFC* with a time of 70 minutes, so it is not possible, even with *B* omitted.

   (c) The minimum connector is now, in order from *A*, *AE*, *ED*, *EF*, *FB*, *BC*, so the route from *A* to *C* is *AEFBC* with a total time of 50 minutes, and a cost of £57.

8 (a)
	A	B	C	D	E	F	G
A	–	23	20	–	–	–	–
B	23	–	–	12	13	–	–
C	20	–	–	16	–	–	28
D	–	12	16	–	–	11	12
E	–	13	–	–	–	9	–
F	–	–	–	11	9	–	12
G	–	–	28	12	–	12	–

   (b) In order, *AC*, *CD*, *DF*, *FE*, *DB*, *DG* or *FG*

   (c) 80

9 (a) *BD*, *BF*, *AB* and *CF*, *BE*   (b) 52 miles

10 (a) $n − 1$

   (b) (i) *AP*, *PH*, *AS*, *SR*, *RW*   (ii) 15 miles

11 (a) *CD*, *EF*, *CF*, *FG*, *BC*, *AB*; length 110

(b) Delete *AF*, *BD*, *BG*, *AG*

Keep *AB*, *BC*, *FG*

Delete *DE*

Keep *CF*, *EF*, *CD*

This also finds a minimum connector.

4 Finding the shortest path

Questions (page 51)

1 St. Albans – Oxford – Swindon – Bristol, 175 km

2 St. Albans – Slough – Oxford – Cheltenham, 1 hour 39 minutes

3 St. Albans – Slough – Swindon – Bristol, 1 hour 56 minutes

Exercise 4 (page 54)

1 *ADFG*, length 13. The labels on *G* are successively 15, 14, 13.

2 *ACDGIJ*, length 19

3 *ACDF*, £40

4

0	1	2	3	6
7	6	3	4	5
8	5	4	5	6
9	12	11	12	7
10	11	10	9	8

5 (a)

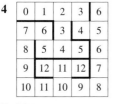

(b) It finds the minimum number of edges needed to link vertex *m* to vertex *n*.

(c) Moore's algorithm is a special case of Dijkstra's algorithm when all edges have weight 1.

Miscellaneous exercise 4 (page 56)

1 (a) *ACEF*, length 9

(b) *ACDF*, length 8. *D* is permanently labelled before *ACD* is considered.

2 (a) *AEOD*, 110 minutes

(b) Add 10 to the numbers on each edge at *O*. *ABCD*, 120 minutes

3 (a) By applying the algorithm from *N*.

(b) *ADFKN*, length 8; *BEGIKN*, length 8, *CEGIKN*, length 7. *C* is nearest.

4 (a) *AD* costs £35; *AE* costs £30; *ADC* costs £55; *AEB* costs £85

(b) *AB* is best, cost £90; other routes unaltered.

5 (a) 8 tons

(b) Replace '*D* + the weight of the edge joining *X* to *Y* ' by 'the greater of *D* and the weight of the edge joining *X* to *Y* '.

6 *ABDEHI*, length 19

7 $1+2+1+2+2+1+2+1+2+2 = 16$

8 (a) *ADEFG*, 110 minutes

(b) Add 5 minutes to each edge through *A* and *G*. Add 10 minutes to each other edge. *ABFG*, 135 minutes

9 (b) In order, *U*, 3; *S*, 4; *T*, 5; then *C*, 6 and *L*, 6 in either order.

(c) Connect *HU*, *US*, *UT*, *TL*, *SC*; cost £9000.

(d) It is a minimum connector, and either Prim's or Kruskal's algorithm would have done.

10 (a) *ACDEG*. Order of labelling, *C*, *D* or *B* in any order, then *F*, *E* and *G*

(b) *A*(*B*)*D*(*F*)*G*   (c) 3 minutes

11 (a) *ADCEFB*, 160 metres. Order of labelling, *A*, *D*, *C*, *E*, *F*, *G*, *B*

(b) Route *ADCEFB* + *BG* + *GECDA*. Length = 335 metres.

12 (b) (i) $9+x$, $8+2x$, $3+3x$ (ii) $1 < x < 3$

5 Matching

Exercise 5 (page 64)

1 (a)

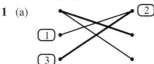

The initial matching cannot be improved.

(b)

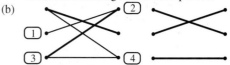

A complete matching is on the right.

2   *R S T U*

$$\begin{array}{c}A\\B\\C\\D\end{array}\begin{pmatrix}1 & 1 & 1 & 0\\1 & 0 & 0 & 1\\0 & 1 & 1 & 0\\1 & 0 & 0 & 1\end{pmatrix}$$

A matching is {*A*,*S*}, {*B*,*R*}, {*C*,*T*}, {*D*,*U*}.

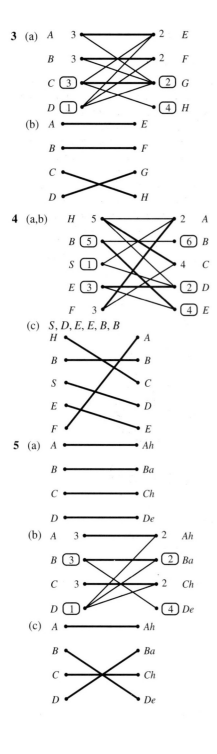

3 (a)

A 3 •———————• 2 E
B 3 •———————• 2 F
C ③ •———————• ② G
D ① •———————• ④ H

(b)

A •———————• E
B •———————• F
C •   ✕   • G
D •———————• H

4 (a,b)

H 5 •———————• 2 A
B ⑤ •———————• ⑥ B
S ① •———————• 4 C
E ③ •———————• ② D
F 3 •———————• ④ E

(c) S, D, E, E, B, B

H •———————• A
B •———————• B
S •———————• C
E •———————• D
F •———————• E

5 (a)

A •———————• Ah
B •———————• Ba
C •———————• Ch
D •———————• De

(b)

A 3 •———————• 2 Ah
B ③ •———————• ② Ba
C 3 •———————• 2 Ch
D ① •———————• ④ De

(c)

A •———————• Ah
B •   • Ba
C •   ✕   • Ch
D •   • De

Miscellaneous exercise 5 (page 67)

1 (a)

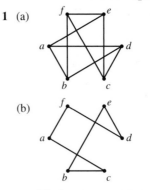

(b)

The lecturer can pair up vertices in successive pairs round the cycle of graph (b). (a,c), (b,e), (d,f).

2 (a,b)

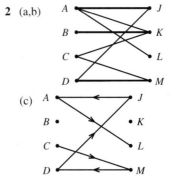

A •———————• J
B •———————• K
C •———————• L
D •———————• M

(c)

A •———————• J
B •   • K
C •   • L
D •———————• M

Arnold pairs with Lorna, Barry with Kate, Charles with Marie, and Derek with Jane.

3 (a)

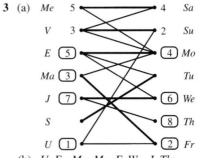

Me   5 •———————• 4   Sa
V   3 •———————• 2   Su
E   ⑤ •———————• ④   Mo
Ma   ③ •———————•   Tu
J   ⑦ •———————• ⑥   We
S   •———————• ⑧   Th
U   ① •———————• ②   Fr

(b) U, Fr, Ma, Mo, E, We, J, Th;
Sa − Me, Su −V, Mo − Ma, Tu − S, We − E, Th − J, Fr − U

4 (a)

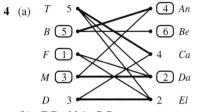

(b) *F Da M An B Be*
Teddy bear - Cathy
Book - Ben
Football - Daniel
Money box - Annie
Drum - Elvis

5 (a)

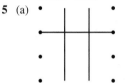

(b) For example, $A - T, B - U, C - S$
(c) 3, because maximum matching = minimum cover

6 (a) If the edge is in the matching, then see part (d). If it not in the matching, then any labelling of the left-vertex would be extended to one for the right-vertex.
(b) All left-vertices which do not belong to the matching are labelled by Step 2 of the algorithm.
(c) If a labelled right-vertex were not in the matching, then the Matching Augmentation algorithm could be used to improve upon this maximum matching.
(d) If an edge of the matching has a labelled right-vertex, then its left-vertex can be labelled with a distance of at most 1 more. If an edge of the matching has a labelled left-vertex, then the labelling has to be 1 more than the labelling of the right-vertex.

6 Route inspection

Exercise 6A (page 73)

1 (a) A closed trail containing every road enters each intersection the same number of times as it leaves the intersection and therefore contributes an even number to the order of each intersection. Each intersection of odd order must therefore be made even by duplicating some roads.
(b) Total of original roads is 1690 metres.
$IH + GC = 340$ m; $IG + HC = 440$ m; $IC + HG = 320$ m which is least, so shortest distance is $(1690 + 320)$ m $= 2010$ m.
(c) All twice, except for E and either B or F which are passed through three times.
(d) 2010 m; the original closed trail passes through all the intersections and is therefore the shortest route for any starting point.

2 (a) (i)

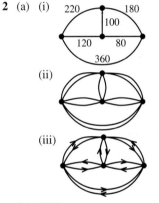

(ii)

(iii)

(b) 1060 m
(c) (i) 1360 m   (ii) 2120 m
(iii) 2120 m

3 Represent rooms by vertices and doorways as edges. Four edges need to be repeated.

4 (a) The row is: 4, $4n-8$, $(n-2)^2$.

        $2n-4$ need to be repeated.

    (b) $2n-2$

Exercise 6B (page 75)

1 (a) Cannot be done as it has two odd vertices.

    (b) Can be done as all the vertices are even.

2 (a) 25 km is the sum of the lengths of all the roads.

    (b) The pairings AC, FG give 5 km;

        AF, CG give 11 km;

        AG, CF give 9 km.

        5 km is lowest, so distance is $(25+5)$ km $= 30$ km.

3 (a) HBC, length 23; HD, length 16; HFE, length 24

    (b)

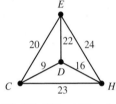

    (c) EF, FH, CD; additional weight $24+9=33$

4 (a) There are seven ways of pairing the first vertex. For each of these seven ways, there are 15 ways of pairing the remaining six vertices; $7 \times 15 = 105$ ways.

    (b) For n odd vertices, $1 \times 3 \times \ldots \times (n-1)$

5 (a) 3770 m   (b) 4520 m

6 Ld – Sh, N – Le, Bi – Br

7 EF and ABC must be repeated.

    One path is $ABCEFEDFGBDCBA$.

Miscellaneous exercise 6 (page 77)

1 (a) All the vertices have odd order. To start and finish at A, they must all be of even order, so some edges must be repeated. Two will need to be repeated.

    (b) Best pairing is $AC + BD = 27$ km.

        Total distance is $(86+27)$ km $= 113$ km.

        One route is $ABDACBDCA$.

    (c) None. All the vertices have order 4 so no pairings are needed.

2 (a) Each edge joins two vertices, so the number of edge ends is even. Suppose that there are r even vertices, and s odd vertices, and that s is odd. Then the total number of edge ends is odd, a contradiction! So the number of odd vertices is even.

    (b) The best pairing of odd vertices is $CE + FI$ totalling 1000 metres. The total inspection route is therefore 6900 metres.

3 (a) Repeat edges AX, BZ and CY; length of route is 86 km.

    (b) Adding AX, BZ and CY takes 2 additions but there are 6 of these. There are 8 additions to find the total length of the edges, and finally these two need to be added to find the total length of the route.

    (c) $AV + BW + CX + DY + EZ$ gives 4 additions, and there are $5 \times 4 \times 3 \times 2 \times 1 = 120$ of these. 25 edges give 24 additions, plus 1 to find the total length of the route.

    (d) There are $n!$ sets, where $n! = 1 \times 2 \times \ldots \times n$, of $n-1$ additions, plus $n^2 - 1$ additions for the n^2 edges, plus 1 to find the total length of the route, giving $n!(n-1)+n^2$ additions.

4 (a) (i) $BG\ SW$, $BS\ GW$, $BW\ GS$

        (ii) 93 miles

    (b) 15   (c) $1 \times 3 \times 5 \times \ldots \times (n-1)$

5 (a) 2800 metres   (b) 4600 metres

    (c) No

6 (a) 180 metres, $ABEBCDEFA$

    (b) (i) $ABEBCRSRYSDEFQPQXPA$

        $(200+10\pi)$ metres

        (ii) B or E

7 (a) There are odd vertices.

    (b) $BD\ FG$, $BF\ DG$, $BG\ DF$

    (c) 5.5, 2.5, 5.5

    (d) $ABFBCEFGEGDEDCA$, 22 miles

8 (a) (i) CD, DE, EF

        (ii) $ABCDEDCEFEBFA$

        (iii) $ABEBCDECBFEFA$

    (b) By starting at C or F

7 The travelling salesperson problem

Exercise 7 (page 85)

1 (a) $ABCDA$, $ABDCA$, $ACBDA$

    (b) $ADCBDA$

2 Calais – Orléans – Poitiers – Bordeaux – Toulouse – Marseille – St-Etienne – Lyons – Dijon – Calais; total 2632 km

3 Pembroke Bay – St Sampson Harbour – St Peter Port – St Martin – Airport – Pleinmont Tower – Perelle Bay – Saline Bay – Soumarez Park – Pembroke Bay; total 22 miles

4 (a) £360

    (b) From C or D, the total is £350.

    (c) B

Miscellaneous exercise 7 (page 89)

1 (a) In each case the lower bound is 30.
  (b) 34
  (c) 34 is only possible if the edges have weights 4, 5, 8, 8, 9. But the edges of weight 4 and 5 form a cycle with one of the edges of weight 8.
  (d) $4 + 5 + 9 + 8 + 9 = 35$

2 The units are kilometres.
  (a) $80 + 110 + 230 + 90 + 90 + 110 + 140 = 850$
  (b) $170 + 110 + 135 + 90 + 90 + 110 + 140 = 845$
  (c) $(170 + 110) + (80 + 90 + 90 + 100 + 110)$
$$= 750$$
$750 \leqslant \text{optimum} \leqslant 845$

3 (a) $\left. \begin{pmatrix} 40 + 72 + 54 + 67 + \\ 61 + 157 + 138 + \\ 122 + 123 + 150 \end{pmatrix} \right|$ miles = 984 miles
  (b) $\left. \begin{pmatrix} 40 + 54 + 61 + \\ 61 + 68 + 72 + \\ 138 + 150 \end{pmatrix} \right|$ miles = 644 miles
  (c) The optimum solution is between 889 and 984 miles.

4 (a) (b) (c)
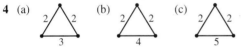

5 (a) *MEABCDM* giving a cost of £81;
      AEMCD – not possible;
      EABMCDE giving a cost of £77
  (b) $£(12 + 13) + £(11 + 12 + 13 + 14) = £75$
      $£75 \leqslant \text{cost} \leqslant £77$
  (c) No effect on the path. The cost of each possible path will be increased by £125.

6 *AEMCD*(via *M* or *C*)*BA*,
  $£(11 + 12 + 13 + 14 + 30 + 12) = £92$

7 (a) *ABCDEA*, 200 minutes
  (b) Smallest pair of in and out edges is
      $B \rightarrow A \rightarrow E$ taking 60 minutes.
      Minimum connector for *B, C, D, E* is
      $20 + 20 + 30$ minutes.
      Total is 130 minutes.
  (c) *EBCDAE*, 150 minutes

8
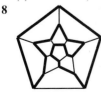

9
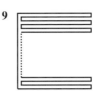

10 Colour the vertices in a chequerboard pattern of black and white. Then white vertices are directly connected only to black vertices and vice versa. Any closed trail must therefore have an even number of vertices. A Hamiltonian cycle would have an odd number n^2 of vertices, so it is not possible.

11 (a) Starting from *H*, Prim's algorithm chooses, in order, *HG, HI, IF, GE, GD, DC, CA, CB*. The length of this route is 720 metres.
   (b) The worst situation occurs when you have to follow the minimum connector out and back to visit all vertices. This, an upper bound, is twice the length of the minimum connector, namely 1440 metres.
   (c) A better route is *HGDCABEFIH*, of length 880 metres.

12 (a) *EY, BC, CD, DE, DZ, AX, AB*. Length 47
   (b) 94
   (c) *ZDCBAXEYZ*. Length 64
   (d) $(9 + 14) + (38) = 61$
   (e) $61 \leqslant L \leqslant 64$

13 (a)
LOVRMCL	175
OVRMCLO	175
COVRMLC	172
MROVLCM	175

   (b) $\begin{matrix} 35 \\ 25 \\ 20 \\ 25 \\ 22 \\ 25 \end{matrix} \begin{pmatrix} - & 5 & 0 & 0 & 7 & 5 \\ 5 & - & 0 & 1 & 5 & 15 \\ 0 & 25 & - & 10 & 15 & 14 \\ 10 & 15 & 5 & - & 15 & 0 \\ 3 & 13 & 0 & 8 & - & 8 \\ 5 & 15 & 9 & 0 & 10 & - \end{pmatrix}$

   (c)
$\begin{matrix} 0 & 5 & 0 & 0 & 5 & 0 \\ \end{matrix}$
$\begin{pmatrix} - & 0 & 0 & 0 & 2 & 5 \\ 5 & - & 0 & 1 & 0 & 15 \\ 0 & 20 & - & 10 & 10 & 14 \\ 10 & 10 & 5 & - & 10 & 0 \\ 3 & 8 & 0 & 8 & - & 8 \\ 5 & 10 & 9 & 0 & 5 & - \end{pmatrix}$

   (d) $35 + 25 + 20 + 25 + 22 + 25 + 5 + 5 = 162$
       VLRMCOV   168

8 Linear programming

Exercise 8A (page 98)

1 (a) y↑

2

0   3   6   x $x_{max} = 3$, $y_{max} = 2$

(b) y↑

4
3

0   4   x $x_{max} = 2$, $y_{max} = 3$

(c) y↑

4
3

0   3   x $x_{max} = 7$, $y_{max} = 4$

(d) y↑

5

0   4   5   x $x_{max} = 4.8$, $y_{max} = 5$

2 (a) 5 at $(3,1)$ (b) 7 at $(1,3)$
    (c) 15 at $(7,4)$ (d) 10 at $(0,5)$

3 5 at $(2,7)$

4 -4 at $(5,1)$

5 9 at anywhere on the line segment from $(2,3)$ to $(0,9)$

Exercise 8B (page 103)

1 (a) Maximise $7x + 8y$, subject to the constraints
$3x + 4y \leq 2400$, $x \leq 400$, $y \leq 400$,
$x, y \geq 0$ are integers.
   (b) £5200 at $(400,300)$

2 £170 at $(10,40)$

3 (a) $p < 2.5$ (b) $p > 10$

4 (a) Maximise $P = x + y$, subject to
$2x + 4y \leq 160$, $5x + 2y \leq 200$, $x \geq 0$,
$y \geq 0$.
   (b) Make 30 of item 1 and 25 of item 2.
   (c) To maximise the profit, make 40 of item 1.

5 (a) $15\frac{5}{17}$ at $\left(2\frac{6}{17}, 3\frac{9}{17}\right)$ (b) 15 at $(0,5)$

6 (a) Maximise $2x + 1.7y$, subject to the
constraints $y \leq 1.52x$, $y \geq 0.8x$, $x \leq 5000$,
$y \leq 3000$, $x \geq 0, y \geq 0$.

(b) Use 3750 kg of X, and 3000 kg of Y for a profit of £12,600.

7 (a) Maximise x, subject to the constraints
$5y \geq 7x$, $x + y \leq 10\,000$, $x, y \geq 0$.
   (b) Invest £4167 in a savings account and £5833 in shares.

8 5 advertisements for the newspapers and 8 for the radio. The cost is £10,000 and the audience is 344 000.

9 Maximise
$P = 1.25x + 0.9y + 0.68z + 2.25u + 1.9v + 1.68w$,
subject to $x + u \leq 5000$, $y + v \leq 10\,000$,
$z + w \leq 10\,000$, $0.7x \leq 0.3(y + z)$,
$0.6y \geq 0.4(x + z)$, $0.6v \leq 0.4(u + w)$,
$0.7w \geq 0.3(u + v)$.

Miscellaneous exercise 8 (page 105)

1 (a) $44\frac{4}{9}$ ml and $66\frac{2}{3}$ ml
   (b) $133\frac{1}{3}$ ml and $233\frac{1}{3}$ ml

2 (a) 14.47 at $(3.71, 2.35)$
   (b) 14 at $(4,2)$ and $(7,0)$

3 (b) That the past is a guide to the future.
   (c) The pensioner should invest £10,000 in deposits, £20,000 in gilts and £40,000 in equities.

4 (a) y↑

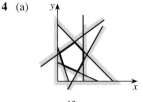

x

(b) (i) $4\frac{12}{17}$ (ii) 7

5 (c) $(0,0)$, $(5000,0)$, $(4500,500)$,
$\left(\frac{24000}{7}, \frac{6000}{7}\right)$; the corresponding values of
P are £0, £20 million, £21 million,
£19 million.
   (d) There should be 4500 UK students and 500 overseas students.

6 (a) $6x + 3y \leq 60$, $3x + 4y \leq 60$, $x \geq 0$, $y \geq 0$
   (b) y↑

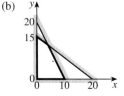

20
15

0   10   20   x

(c) The company should make 4 Brainy and 12 Superbrainy robots.

7 (a) $100a + 500b + 200c \leqslant 2000$
$a + 4b + 3c \leqslant 50$

(b) $2a + 9b + 5c$

(c) Maximise $P = 2a + 9b + 5c$,
subject to $100a + 500b + 200c \leqslant 2000$,
$a + 4b + 3c \leqslant 50$,
$a \geqslant 0, b \geqslant 0, c \geqslant 0$.

(d) The need for integer solutions.

(e) Use the constraint, $a + 2b + 3c \leqslant 20$.

8 (a) $3x + 2y + z \leqslant 120, 3x + 4y + 6z \leqslant 330$

(b) (i) Set $z = y$

(ii),(iii)

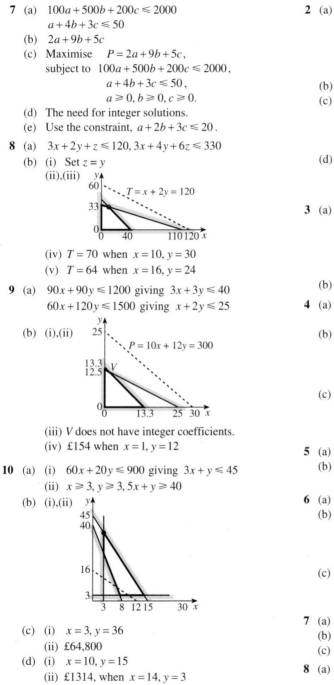

(iv) $T = 70$ when $x = 10, y = 30$

(v) $T = 64$ when $x = 16, y = 24$

9 (a) $90x + 90y \leqslant 1200$ giving $3x + 3y \leqslant 40$
$60x + 120y \leqslant 1500$ giving $x + 2y \leqslant 25$

(b) (i),(ii)

(iii) V does not have integer coefficients.

(iv) £154 when $x = 1, y = 12$

10 (a) (i) $60x + 20y \leqslant 900$ giving $3x + y \leqslant 45$

(ii) $x \geqslant 3, y \geqslant 3, 5x + y \geqslant 40$

(b) (i),(ii)

(c) (i) $x = 3, y = 36$

(ii) £64,800

(d) (i) $x = 10, y = 15$

(ii) £1314, when $x = 14, y = 3$

Revision exercise
(page 110)

1 (a)

X	24	4	4	4	4
Y	20	16	12	8	4

(b) Finds the highest common factor of X and Y.

2 (a)

(b) AC, CD/AB, AE; length 8

(c) $ABCDEA$ (Shortest - 18)
$ABEDCA$ (21)
$ACBEDA$ (28)
$ADCBEA$ (26)

(d) In practice, a salesperson would travel
$ABACDEA$, which does have length
$2 \times$ minimum connector.

3 (a) Maximise $80c + 350t$,
subject to $4c + 15t \leqslant 1950$,
$c + 5t \leqslant 500$,
$c \geqslant 0, t \geqslant 0$.

(b) $c = 450, t = 10$. Income = £39,500

4 (a) G1 does not; there is no AD link.
G2 requires 55 lines.

(b)

31 lines

(c)

30 lines
The 'greedy' first choice of AC proves not to
be best over all.

5 (a) $AEBFGHJKMN$, 26 miles

(b) FI reduces only AI.
DJ reduces AJ, AK, AL, AM, AN.

6 (a) B, F, D, G

(b) There are odd vertices whereas Eulerian
graphs have all vertices even, because the
number of edges 'in' must equal the number
of edges 'out' at each vertex.

(c) Repeat BF and DEG.
For example, $ABFBCEFGEDEGDCA$
2200 miles

7 (a) AB, BC, BD (or CD), CE, EF

(b) 33 miles

(c) Cycles are hard to spot from the matrix.

8 (a)

(b) C–Mon, F–Tue, G–Wed, P–Mon, Stop

(c) C–Mon, F–Tue, G–Wed, P–Tue, R–Mon

9 $ABEDC$ Weight 52

10 (a) 3 (b) 15

(c) $19 \times 17 \times 15 \times \ldots \times 3 = 654\,729\,075$

11 (a) $4! = 24$

(b) $49! = 6.08 \times 10^{62}$, 1.9×10^{48} years

12 (a) $50(450x + 600y) \le 450\,000$ or $3x + 4y \le 60$

$100(200x + 150y) \le 300\,000$ or $4x + 3y \le 60$

(b)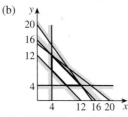

(c) £120,000; $(4,8)$, $(5,7)$, $(6,6)$, $(7,5)$, $(8,4)$

(d) Profit (£) is $S(x + y) - 42\,500x - 45\,000y$.

This is maximum when $x + y = 16$.

$S_{MAX} = 56\,250$ at $(4,12)$,

$S_{MIN} = 55\,000$ at $(12,4)$.

13 $BD, BF, BA/CF, BE$. Cost £525

14 (a)

A	0	216	449.28	701.22
I		1	2	3

(b) Interchange the last two lines.

(c) $A = F$

INPUT N, P, R

FOR $I = 1$ TO N

$A = A + P$

$A = \left(1 + \frac{1}{100}R\right) \times A$

NEXT I

PRINT A

Mock examinations

Mock examination 1 (page 116)

1 (a) BD, BF, BE, AD, CF (b) 52 miles

2 (a,b)

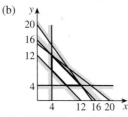

$Ch–I, S–R, Pe–A, Cl–P$

3 (a) $AECD$, 5 minutes   (b) $1 \le x < 3$

4 CFADBHEG

BFADCHEG

ADBFCGEH

ABCDEFGH

$4 + 7 + 12 = 23$ comparisons

5 (a) $BACDB$, 290 minutes

(b) $(40 + 110) + 60 = 210$ minutes

(c) $ACBDA$, 270 minutes (minimal)

$ABCDA$, 280 minutes

$ABDCA$, 290 minutes

(d) $ABACADA$, 200 minutes

It is better to repeat edges from A than to use direct links between B, C and D.

6 (a) Minimise $R = 24\,000x + 30\,000y$,

subject to $x + y \ge 200$,

$7x + 9y \ge 1500$,

$x \le 300$,

$y \le 150$.

(b,c)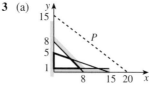

At $(150, 50)$, $R = $ £5.1M

(d) By £857

Mock examination 2 (page 118)

1 (a)

A	2	2	2	2.125
B	3	2.5	2.25	2.25
D	2.5	2.25	2.125	2.1875

(b) Find the cube root of C.

(c) No stopping condition, and no output.

2 (a) For example, $ABCFEDCFEGFBGA$, 9700 m

(b) CE, so every vertex has even order.

(c) 1450 m

3 (a)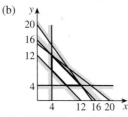

(b) $P = 27.5$ at $(4.5, 3.5)$

(c) At $(5, 3)$

4

9	7	5	5	2	2	2	2
7	9	7	7	5	5	5	5
5	5	9	9	7	7	6	6
13	13	13	13	9	8	7	7
2	2	2	2	13	9	8	8
8	8	8	8	8	13	9	9
6	6	6	6	6	6	13	13
16	16	16	16	16	16	16	16

5 (c) 6   (d) (i) 72   (ii) $\frac{1}{2}(n-1)!n!$

6 (a) 115

(b) Perform a reverse pass, using edges whose weights equal the differences in the permanent labels of the vertices they join. *ACEHIG*

(c) *RSU* has length 4; *RSVU* has length $2+x$.

(d) $2+2x$, $4+x$, 7

(i) $x<2$ (ii) $2<x<3$ (iii) $x>3$

Glossary

Algorithm	A finite sequence of instructions for solving a problem.
Bipartite graph	A graph with two sets of vertices such that edges only connect vertices from one set to the other.
Complete graph, K_n	A simple graph such that each of its n vertices is directly connected by an edge to every other vertex.
Connected graph	A graph such that there is a path between any two vertices of the graph.
Cycle	A closed trail where only the initial and final vertices are the same.
Digraph	A graph with directed edges.
Eulerian graph	A connected graph which has a closed trail containing every edge precisely once.
Euler's relationship	$R + V = E + 2$
Graph	A set of points (called vertices or nodes) joined by lines (called edges or arcs).
Greedy algorithm	An algorithm where the immediately 'best' step is made without concern about the long-term consequences of this choice.
Hamiltonian cycle	A cycle which passes through every vertex of the graph.
Matching	A set of edges which have no vertices in common.
Minimum connector	A spanning tree whose edges have minimum possible total weight.
Network	A graph with numbers (called weights) associated with its edges.
Order (of a vertex)	The number of edges meeting at that vertex.
Path	A trail such that no vertex is passed through more than once.
Planar graph	A graph which can be drawn in a plane in such a way that edges only meet at vertices.

Semi-Eulerian graph	A connected graph with a trail which is not closed that contains every edge precisely once.
Simple graph	A graph without loops or multiple edges.
Spanning tree	A subgraph which is a tree connecting all the vertices of the graph.
Subgraph of G	A graph whose vertices and edges are all in the graph G.
Trail	A sequence of edges such that the end vertex of one edge is the start vertex of the next.
Travelling salesperson problem	The classical problem of finding a Hamiltonian cycle of minimum possible weight. (In the practical problem, vertices and edges may be revisited.)
Tree	A connected graph with no cycles.

Summary of algorithms

Problem	Name of algorithm
Sorting	Bubble Sort
	Shell Sort
	Quicksort
	Shuttle Sort
Matching	Matching Augmentation
Minimum connector	Prim's
	Kruskal's
Shortest path	Dijkstra's
Route inspection	Chinese Postman
Travelling salesperson	Nearest Neighbour
	Lower Bound
	Tour Improvement
Linear programming	Graphical

Index

The page numbers given refer to the first mention of each term, or the shaded box if there is one.